The Seventh Flag

Comanche Indians in Texas

By

John Proctor

© 2001 by John Proctor. All rights reserved.

No part of this book may be reproduced, stored in a retrieval system, or transmitted by any means, electronic, mechanical, photocopying, recording, or otherwise, without written permission from the author.

ISBN: 0-7596-7464-7

This book is printed on acid free paper.

1stBooks - rev. 01/05/02

Table of Contents

PREFACE

American Indians played a significant role in American history and in shaping the United States. American history often overlooks our Indian heritage. Historian Frances Parkman stated, "Spanish civilization crushed the Indian; English civilization scorned and neglected him; French civilization embraced and cherished him."[1] Americans like their English cousins continued with the same view toward Indians.

Most Americans believe our history would be essentially the same whether nor not Indians were present. Nothing could be farther from the truth. Texas, in particular, was significantly influenced by the presence of the Comanche Indians.

About 1800, a Spanish general proclaimed, "Texas is the key to all New Spain."[2] The Comanche Indians, though, possessed that key. After several encounters, Spain soon realized that the Comanches were the real masters of the Texas interior. One Spanish governor of Texas reported that his presidio troopers quailed at the mere mention of the Comanches.

Spain, skilled in political relationships, would come to exploit the Comanches to their advantage. If Spain could not enter Comanche territory, neither could Britain nor France, the principal Spanish rivals. In this way the Comanches became a two-edged sword. The Comanches would prevent all intruders, Spaniards or anyone else, from

---

[1] Rollings, 7
[2] Editors of Time-Life Books, 93

entering into Texas, and, therefore, become a buffer to protect New Mexico and Northern Mexico. Spain was also successful in enlisting the aid of the Comanches in fighting their common enemy, the Apaches.

In the recording of Texas history, little is said of the influence the Comanches had in the development of Texas. They appear only as savages that should be scorned as only an aggravation like wild aggressive animals and in no way equal to the nations representing the six flags over Texas. They were, however, successful in holding at bay the Spaniards and Mexicans. As a result, Texas was then opened for settlement by Americans. The Spanish and later the Mexicans believed American immigrants in Texas would neutralize Comanche raids into Mexico. American settlements in Texas would create more nearby targets for Comanche raiders and, therefore, the Comanches would have no need to raid more distant Mexico.

I

The Lure of the Orient

Most historians conclude that the story of America had its genesis in the Crusades. In all, there were eight Crusades, which were carried out over two centuries. Only the first seemed to have a measure of success.

Around the year 1090, the Christian Byzantium Empire was being threatened by the Muslim Turks.[3] To counter this threat, the Byzantium emperor warned the Christian kingdoms in Europe that the Turks had closed access to the holy places in Palestine. Pope Urban II then encouraged European noblemen to form a crusade and travel to the Holy Land and protect it. The First Crusade, 1096-1099, resulted in the capture of Jerusalem. The Turks, however, counterattacked, and in subsequent battles the Christians were driven from the Holy Land. Their final exit was in 1291.

Although the Crusades was a failure, the Europeans came away with a new knowledge of the East. They found new foods, textiles, ad scientific skills.[4] Of particular interest to the Europeans were cane sugar, buckwheat, rice, apricots, watermelons, oranges, limes, lemons, cotton, damask, satin, velvet and dyestuffs. The East also showed the Europeans a superior civilization such as large cities,

---

[3] Compton's Home Library, Crusades Pope Urban II encouraged European noblemen: National Geographic Society, 138
[4] Compton's Home Library, Crusades the Silk Road...: National Geographic Society, 75

splendid buildings, highly-developed arts and crafts, medical skills and scientific knowledge.

The Crusades was not the first exposure of Eastern culture to the Europeans. The Europeans were trading gold, wool, horses, and glass for silk that came from China over the Silk Road, which began about 2 BC. This was a 4000-mile overland road that originated in Xian, China and ended at eastern Mediterranean ports. From here, ships brought silk to Europe in exchange for European goods. Silk, at the time, was worth its weight in gold.

Marco Polo with his father and uncle also traveled to China. Marco Polo was in China about the time of the last Crusade. He remained in China for several years and became well acquainted with China's leaders. He returned to Venice and wrote his famous narratives of his adventures. These narratives heightened Europeans' interest in the Orient.[5]

This new knowledge was the spark, or awakening, to bring Europe out of the Age of Feudalism. The feudal system had acted as a brake on European development. The feudal system was characterized by petty kingdoms that were constantly at war with one another. Feudalism largely disappeared from Western Europe in 1400, which opened the way for fresh ideas.[6]

The new awakening in Europe centered on two concepts: The Age of Discovery and the Renaissance. The Renaissance began in Italy as early as 1300, and from here it spread gradually to other parts of Europe. Formerly,

---

[5] Ibid., 126
[6] Compton's Home Library, Feudalism Age of Discovery and Renaissance: National Geographic Society, 150

European thought adhered to a church-centered perspective. Afterwards, the Europeans developed a passion for change and new directions that became contagious. Painting, architecture, writing, religion, politics, and daily lives were caught up in the passion for change. This in turn strengthened a passion for exploration and ultimately the Age of Discovery.

It seemed, however, that the Ottoman Turks had deliberately planned to extinguish the Europeans' passion for exploration. The Turks were Muslim who, as they believed, had a duty to wage war against Christian Europe. In 1453, Constantinople and the Byzantine Empire fell to the Turks. Their expanding empire extended from Buda in Central Europe to Basra in Asia. They also created a powerful navy that controlled the coastline along the Persian Gulf, Red Sea, Eastern Mediterranean Sea and most of the North African Coast. The Turkish Empire set astride the junction of three continents. The Silk Road was then closed to Europeans.[7]

Before 1500, travel had been land centered. Ships would only travel within sight of land. However, it was not until 1488 that Bartholomeu Dias, a Portugese sailor, proved that it was possible to sail around the coast of Africa.[8] Once around Africa, spices and silks could readily be obtained from the Orient.

The voyage around Africa, though, was long and perilous. Portugal, though, was unable to immediately capitalize on Dias' find. It was not until 1497 that Vasco

---

[7] Ibid., 154
[8] Ibid., 151

da Gama with four ships sailed around Africa.[9] The voyage took more than two years; the loss of two ships and the loss of half the crew. Thereupon, businessmen and traders sought a better way to get to the Orient.

The Renaissance not only produced changes in philosophical thought but also technical knowledge. Navigational technology was improved; so that Europeans were emboldened to venture into open seas out of sight of land. Price Henry, "the Navigator" of Portugal, improved ships' design with multiple masts and sturdy sails.[10] The navigational instruments, at the time, included the sandglass, compass, lodestone, and astrolabe. The astrolabe was the forerunner of the Sextant.[11] By sighting astronomical bodies, sailors could determine their location by knowing how far south or north they were. The compass had been invented by the Chinese two centuries earlier but was new to the Europeans. Prince Henry also made improvements to the compass.

Prince Henry, the third son of King John I of Portugal, also set up a naval school at Sagres, Portugal.[12] One of his students was a sailor from Genoa, Italy: Christopher Columbus. Columbus gained considerable experience by sailing along the coast of Europe and Africa. In time, Columbus became convinced that one could reach the Orient by sailing west across the Atlantic.

Columbus then advanced a request to the king of Portugal to sponsor a voyage west.[13] The king turned down

---

[9] Ibid., 168
[10] Ibid., 166
[11] Ibid., 179
[12] Ibid., 166
[13] Ibid., 166

his request for ships. Columbus then went to the court of King Ferdinand and Queen Isabella of Spain to present his request for ships. The Spanish royalty categorically denied Columbus' request in 1487.

Spain, at the time, was battling the Moor invader from Africa. The Moors or Muslim Arabs entered Spain through Gibraltar in the eighth century and occupied Spain for almost eight hundred years. In the last half of the Moors' occupation, Spain rose-up to drive the Moors from Spain. The Spanish campaign reached the pinnacle of success in 1469 when the two largest states in the Spanish kingdom were united by the marriage of Ferdinand of Aragon and Isabella of Castile.[14] This united force then drove the last Moor from their remaining stronghold in Granada in 1492.

Encouraged by this news, Columbus again requested ships from the Spanish monarchy. This time, he was successful and was furnished with three ships. On August 3, 1492, he sailed from Palos, Spain bound for the canary Islands.[15] He left these islands, sailing west, on September 6 and lost all sight of land until October 12. Unknowingly, the Columbus expedition arrived at an island in the Caribbean Sea. Columbus believed he had reached India, and, therefore, the native people on the island must be Indian. This error, no matter how erroneous, was never corrected by Europeans and later Americans. All native people in the Western Hemisphere were accorded the name, Indian.

Columbus returned to Spain in triumph. The news of his voyage was heralded not only in Spain but also all

---

[14] Thomas, 38
[15] National Geographic Society, 167

Europe. Portugal was particularly alarmed, as it believed that Columbus had indeed found a shorter route to Asia. Fearing competition for their Asian routes, which Portugal claimed to own a monopoly, Portugal requested the Pope intercede in its behalf. As both nations were Catholic, the Pope could readily arbitrate their differences. With the Treaty of Tordesillas in 1494 the Pope drew a north-south line on a map of the Atlantic Ocean.[16] The established line was set at 370 leagues west of the Cape Verde Islands. Everything east of this line was Portugese rights, and everything west of the line was the right of Spain. Only present day Brazil was east of the line. Therefore, Spain had the lion's share of rights in the New World.

After driving the Moors from Spain, Spain had a ready pool of trained military manpower to exploit its allotted territory. Conquistadores or conquerors, followed by Jesuit and Franciscan priests, set out from Spain for the three Gs: God, gold, and glory. They setup bases in Cuba, Hispaniola, and Panama. From these bases they readily conquered the Aztec, Mayan, and Inca Empires. These conquests produced vast wealth for Spain. It became Europe's most puissant power. England, France, and the Netherlands were then drawn to the New World to search for opportunities. Also, even more Spanish conquistadores were lured to find their fortunes in the New World.

For three centuries after Columbus' first voyage to the New World, Spain dominated the Western Hemisphere. To consolidate the enormous land area, Spain had to overcome one great problem: it did not have a surplus population. It had excellent soldiers. Cortes conquered the Aztec empire

---

[16] Ibid., 174

with less than 600 men. Spanish immigrants to the New World, though, numbered less than 1,000 per year.[17] Cortes set the mode of Spanish colonization: "I did not come to the New World to till the soil like any peasant."[18] Therefore, Spain concluded that the best way to control its holdings in the New World was to convert the native population to Roman Catholicism, the religion of Spain. Once converted, the native population would automatically become loyal citizens of Spain. The native Indian population would thus be Spain's colonists. They would do the manual labor under the direction of their Spanish overseers.

Therefore, wherever conquistadores ventured, Franciscan, Jesuit, and Dominican missionaries followed. The Indians in Mexico were easily converted after the Aztec empire was conquered. Hispanicization became more difficult, however, as Spain endeavored to push north. Areas to the north held more hostile Indians. Spain then developed the mission-presidio system.[19]

The missionaries were to instruct the Indians in the Catholic faith and to adopt an agricultural way of life. The soldiers in the presidio, or garrison fort, were to protect the missionaries and converted Indians.

In California and New Mexico the Spanish missionary system seemed to succeed. Between 1769 and 1823, Spain constructed 21 missions along the Pacific coast from San Diego northward for 650 miles to San Francisco.[20] For their efforts, the missionaries converted 17,000 Indians.

---

[17] Editors of Time-Life Books, 18
[18] Ibid., 49
[19] Ibid., 49
[20] Ibid., 149

In 1799, the New Mexico province had a Spanish population of 18,826. The leading town in New Mexico, Santa Fe, had a Spanish population of 3, 795. The native Indian population was composed of what the Spanish called Pueblo Indians, as they lived in small adobe brick buildings. These buildings were constructed within communities, and the native population did mostly farm. They grew corn, beans and squash. They were equally adapted to weaving and pottering. When the Spanish first arrived in the area, there were about 40,000 Pueblo Indians living along the upper reaches of the Rio grande River.

In Texas, the Spanish found an entirely different type of Indian. The Indians of Texas were nomadic and had no interest in farming. Every male Indian was a warrior and a hunter. Though, a few docile Indians did exist in the area. These latter Indians were willing converts to the Spanish missionary system. They sought shelter from the nomadic Indians who would enslave them.

In Texas, Spain constructed more than 30 missions.[21] They were, for the most part, failures. None of the Indians from the nomadic tribes would willingly enter a mission. They would not trade their glorious lives as hunters, horsemen and warriors to become farmers. To them, missionary life would be the same as a prison.

The Plains Indians were free men. They were not free in the same sense as present day Americans. They were free as the wind or an eagle. The eagle flies where he will and is only restricted or encumbered by things in nature. Thus, working as a laborer under the tutelage of a Spanish overseer would be tantamount to a death sentence. The

---

[21] Ibid., 94

Indians south of the Rio Grande, on the other hand, merely traded one despot for another. They were then easily persuaded to till the soil and work in mines for their Spanish overseers.

At one time, there were about 12 Indian tribes in Texas. The most significant were the Apache, Comanche, Cherokee, Kiowa, Wichita, Caddo, Coahuiltecan, Karankawa and Tonkawa. Of these, the Comanche stands out as the dominant tribe in Texas.

Before the arrival of horses to the New World, the Comanche Indians were only a wretched band of Indians who lived on the edge of survival. Dogs and women were used as pack animals. Game animals, although plentiful in the area, were not readily harvested, as they could only be obtained through stealth by a hunter on foot.

Between 1650 and 1750, Spanish horses began to arrive on the plains of Texas. With the horse, the Comanches became the dominant people of the Texas plains. For most of the 18th and 19th centuries, the Comanches kept at bay all intruders of their territory, Indian or European. The Comanche's territory, which the Spanish called the Comancheria, encompassed an area over 24,000 square miles.[22] It extended from the Arkansas River in Colorado and Kansas southward to include most of Oklahoma, Eastern New Mexico, and West Texas. Its southern limit was approximately at the junction of the Pecos and Rio grande Rivers in Texas.

One consequence of Comanche domination in Texas was its effect on travelers. To travel from the Spanish

---

[22] Rollings, 21

settlement at Santa Fe in New Mexico to San Antonio in Texas required a circuitous route south into Coahuila and Chihuahua in Mexico and then north to San Antonio, which about doubled the more direct route.[23] This route, although longer but safer, skirted the Comancheria and, thus, avoided a perilous encounter with the feared Comanche Indians. After many disastrous clashes, Spain realized that the Comanches were the real masters of the Texas interior.

In 1783, almost 300 years after Spain claimed Texas, Spanish Governor Domingo Cabello drew up a census for Texas. The census counted a total population of only 2,819 terrified people. Most of the people lived in San Antonio and a smaller number in La Bahia, now Goliad. This census included not only Spaniards but also docile Indians.

Texas was a wild and dangerous place. Very few Spaniards and later Mexicans dared settle in Texas. Not only their property but also their very lives were at risk. The Comanches, at the time, were the lords of Texas. The most telling evidence of the Comanche influence on the history of Texas is the contrast of Spanish populations in New Mexico and Texas. There were less than 3000 in Texas and almost 19,000 in New Mexico during the same period.[24]

Texas history states that Texas was under six flags:

> Spanish flag: 1519-1821
> French fag: 1685-1691
> Mexican flag: 1821-1836
> Texas flag: 1836-1845

---

[23] Richardson, 23
[24] Editors, 96 & 131

Confederate flag: 1861-1865
United States flag: 1845 to present

Texas history, to be correct, should include a Comanche flag, a seventh flag. The Comanches dominated Texas for almost 200 years between the early 1700s and 1875.

II

Exploration

Once Columbus' discovery of the New World became known in Europe, it set off an era of exploration and colonization that profoundly affected the history of the world. Spain took an early lead. From bases established in Cuba and Hispaniola, Spain sent out conquistadores and missionaries for "God, gold and glory."[25]

Probably the best-known conquistador was Hernando Cortes. He was well known for his military and administrative abilities. In 1519, he sailed from Cuba with an army of 508 soldiers, 17 horses, and 10 cannons to conquer the Aztec Empire, which was a highly civilized nation of 11 million people. The odds of his succeeding were minimal.[26]

Cortes, however, benefitted from an Aztec legend. The year 1519 was the time that Aztec priests prophesied the return of their great god, Quetzalcoatl. After an absence of five centuries, he was to return out of the waters from the east. Cortes seemed to fit the legend. Cortes was also aided by an Aztec noble woman named Malinche whom Cortes called "Donna Marina." She became Cortes' devoted mistress and plotted with him to defeat her own people.

Within three years, Cortes had conquered the Aztec Empire and the adjoining Mayan Empire. From their base

---

[25] Ibid., 19
[26] Ibid., 30

in southern Mexico, Spain easily extended control of most of the continent. The native Indian population was stripped of its gold and forced to work in mines to produce more gold and silver for their Spanish overlords. The great wealth that Cortes brought back from Mexico wetted the appetites of other conquistadores to equal or even excel Cortes. The Cortes expedition further verified legends of gold in the New World. One legend that took roots among the conquistadores was the existence of seven cities of gold. This legend was founded during the Moors' occupation of Spain and Portugal. Seven Christian bishops, to escape persecution by the infidels, sailed across the Sea of Darkness. They landed on an island they named, Antilles. Here, the bishops found large quantities of gold and, thus, built seven cities of gold, one for each bishop.[27]

The conquistadores believed what they wanted to believe. Gold was readily found in the New World, and it was theirs for the taking. Explorers and geographers even named several Caribbean Islands the Antilles after the legendary Antilia. These islands were barren of gold. Therefore, the seven cities of gold must be on the mainland.

Rumors of the seven cities of gold persisted along with the Spaniards insistent desire for gold. The first viceroy of Mexico, Antonio de Mendoza, was finally overcome by the stories of the seven cities of gold. He commissioned a young nobleman, Francisco Vasquez de Coronado, to explore the area north of Mexico.[28] To assist Coronado was a Franciscan friar, Marcos de Niza, who had the

---

[27] Ibid.: 25
[28] Rollings, 17

reputation of being a fearless explorer and skilled cartographer.

Marcos was sent ahead to scout the land and report of his findings. After six months, Marcos returned to Mexico City and reported that he found no evidence of gold. However, in the distance he saw a metropolis "bigger than the city of Mexico." An Indian informed Marcos that farther north, "was much gold, and that the natives in it trade in vessels and jewels for the ears, and little plates with which they scrape themselves and remove the sweat."

Stimulated by this news, Coronado gathered his force to explore the north in February 1540. His army consisted of 300 Spanish soldiers and 800 local Indian warriors. He left his headquarters at Compostela, Mexico near the Pacific coast and traveled northward along the Pacific shore. When he reached present day Arizona, he expected to find a bustling town. Instead, he found only a miserable hovel and most importantly no gold. Coronado and his army were disheartened. However, when they reached a Zuni village, they received good news. The Zunis reported a rich province that lay to the northwest. Again the Spaniards were disappointed, as there was no rich province to the northwest.

While awaiting scouting reports, Coronado was visited by some Indians from Cicuye, a pueblo 200 miles further east. The Spaniards were invited to come to their village. These Indians were, at first, friendly. However, when a Spanish soldier raped an Indian woman, the relationship between the Spaniards and the Indians soured. The Indians then advised the Spaniards that a city of gold, Quivira, was to the north.[29] They furnished the Spaniards a guide who was well acquainted with the region. The Spaniards named him El Turco, because he looked like a Turk.

El Turco led the Spaniards north along the Rio Grande river and then east across the Pecos River. In about two weeks, they reached the open plains. El Turco then led the army southeast and not northeast, as expected, toward Quivira. Coronado and his army arrived in what is now the Texas Panhandle. Here, he came upon some Indians, native to the area, the Tewas. These Indians described Quivira's houses as being made of grass and hides. Coronado then became suspicious of El Turco.

By applying various means of torture, the Spaniards were able to extract the truth from El Turco. The Indian guide confessed that he had lied about the gold. He had conspired with two Cicuye chiefs to lead the Spaniards on a long arduous expedition that would wear-down Coronado's army. The Spaniards would then be easy prey. In retrospect, Coronado realized El Turco reported only what the Spaniards wanted to hear.

Coronado then took the long tortuous journey back to Mexico City. He had been gone for some two and half years. His venture was considered a failure, as he found no gold or silver. Almost forgotten was that Coronado's venture gave the Spanish crown a claim to about the whole of the southwestern part of North America.

About 10 years before the Coronado expedition, Panfilo de Narvaez with 300 men left Cuba and landed on the west coast of Florida.[30] He was instructed to proceed northward

---

[29] editors, 38
[30] Ibid., 26

but after following that order, the Narvaez expedition was never heard from again. It completely disappeared.

A few years after Coronado returned to Mexico City, some Spanish soldiers in northen Mexico came upon four unusual men that were not native to Mexico. It turned out that the four men were from the lost Narvaez expedition. One of the men was Alvar Nunez Cabeza de Vaca, a Spanish aristocrat. Cabeza de Vaca and his companions were escorted back to Mexico City where they were greeted as heroes.

Cabeza de Vaca then told of his wanderings. He and his companions traveled about 6,000 miles. They left Florida in five horsehide boats on the Gulf of Mexico. Shortly thereafter three of the boats sank carrying with them 200 men. The remaining two boasts made a landing on a large sandy island, which was probably Galveston Island. The survivors swam to the mainland where they were found by some friendly Indians. The Indians tried to be helpful, but they probably were in more need than the Spaniards. Gradually the Spaniards died of starvation, disease, malnutrition and exposure. Finally there were only four Spanish survivors remaining.

The four Spaniards and a few Indians then proceeded to travel west. They went through present day Texas, New Mexico and Arizona. Here, they met with Pima Indians. At first, the Spaniards were treated as slaves. Later, they were treated with respect and allowed to travel southward into Mexico. In Mexico, they were found by other Spaniards and eventually returned to Mexico City.

The exploration activities of Coronado and Cabeza de Vaca plus the Treaty of Tordesillas gave Spain an almost undisputed title to most of the western part of present day

United States. Also reinforcing Spain's claim to Texas was Spanish explorer, Alonso Alvarez de Pineda, who charted the Texas coast in 1519.

Unknowingly, French Explorer, La Salle, upset Spanish hegemony in Texas. In 1682, La Salle floated down the Mississippi River to its mouth.[31] There, he claimed all of the Mississippi Valley for King Louis XIV and named it Louisiana. In 1685, he returned with French colonists. However, through navigational error, he missed the mouth of the Mississippi River and instead landed at Matagorda Bay on the coast of Texas. Here, he established a French colony, which he named Fort St. Louis.

When the Spaniards in Mexico City learned of the French settlement, they immediately formed a military expedition to find and destroy it. When the French colony was located, the Spaniards realized that the Indians had done their job for them. The French colony was destroyed and all French colonists were either dead or missing. This was the only attempt by France to establish a claim in Texas.

At the time, Spain and other European countries were not particularly concerned with Texas. Spain's only interest was to prevent other Europeans from encroaching upon Spanish claims. Spain's policy in Texas was one of reaction. It would react only to a foreign incursion.

In 1713, French Canadian Louis Juchereau de St. Denis was commissioned to establish a trading post on the Red River for trade with Indians.[32] The name of the French outpost was Natchitoches. Upon learning of the French

---

[31] Ibid., 55
[32] Ibid., 61

post, the Spanish were driven to action. They constructed an outpost 15 miles from Natchitoches: San Miguel de los Adaes.

In 1719, France declared war on Spain. To bring the war to the enemy, the French force at Natchitoches, consisting of seven soldiers, marched on the Spanish outpost of San Miguel. The Spanish defense consisted of one lay brother and one soldier. The war on the Red River quickly ended. Shortly thereafter, France and Spain were at peace.

The French action, though, moved the Spanish to increase their presence in Texas. Marquis of San Miguel de Aguayo, the soldier-governor of Coahuila, then increased the number of missions in Texas from two to ten,[33] one presidio to four, and a military establishment from 50 to 268 soldiers.

Spain, at the time, was a world power. Its presence extended throughout the world. Texas was left to the jurisdiction of New Spain as Mexico was then called. Even this did not simplify the administration of Texas. Saltillo, the capital of Texas and Coahuila, was 300 miles from San Antonio. Mexico City, the capital of New Spain, was more than 1500 miles from San Antonio.

Mexico City was not just geographically distant. Its people also lived in such opulent comfort that they could not or would not imagine a place so remote as the wild and dangerous frontier of Texas. Politicians, army officers, and businessmen of Mexico City flaunted their wealth. Their wives wore diamonds and gold around their necks with satin slippers on their feet. Thomas Gage, an Englishman

---

[33] Ibid. 62

who visited Mexico City in the 1630s wrote,[34] "It is a byword that at Mexico there is four things fair, that is to say, the women, the apparel, the horses, and the streets. But to this I may add the beauty of some of the coaches of the gentry, which do exceed the cost of the best of the Court of Madrid and other parts of Christendom, for they spare no silver, or gold, nor the best silks from China to enrich them." Mexico City became known as the Paris of the Western Hemisphere.

People in Texas worked the land with their hands and lived in crude shelters. The governing officials and politicians in Mexico City could never relate to the life and problems in Texas. The original goals of Spain in the New World, the three Gs: God, gold, and glory, were reduced to gold only.

Gold was a commodity that could easily be converted to currency. Its value was readily known. Land, on the other hand, was not so easily converted. Spain was mostly interested in developing a steady source of revenue and had little interest in building a colonial empire as the English did in North America. Spain's New World possessions were a captive market and only a source of wealth for Spain. In this end, Spain was successful, as New Spain provided almost two thirds of Spain's revenues at the beginning of the 19th century.[35] Thus, the overriding ambition of Spanish conquistadores was gold. Land that did not have rich agricultural promise or was without mines, was only delineated on a map as Spanish territory;

---

[34] Ibid. 19
[35] Johnson, 45

forgotten or at most a missionary priest was sent to the area.

Theoretically, all property claimed by an expedition belonged to the crown. The explorers, though, acted as agents of the crown, which demanded only a fifth of the revenue generated by the property. This enabled the exploration leaders to reward their followers with land and gold.[36] When gold could not be found in adequate quantities, land was readily available to be disbursed by the exploration leader. Such land was delineated on a map, which was probably inaccurately drawn. There was no title searches or a team of surveyors on hand to define the property. Most of the time, ownership of the land granted in this manner was never physically set out by the owner. The owner never saw his land. The land was held as a commodity that could be exchanged for value when the owner returned to Spain. Consequently, Spanish land grants, especially those in East Texas, are undefinable to this day.

A natural phenomena appeared to reinforce the Spanish lust for gold: the trade winds. These winds blew from the Greater Antilles: Cuba, Hispaniola, Jamaica, and Puerto Rico, directly toward Central America, North Venezuela, Southern Mexico and adjacent Carribean Islands. This area became known as the Spanish Main.

The trade winds seemed to blow from Cuba and Hispaniola directly toward Panama. At Panama, Spanish ships loaded gold obtained from mines in Peru transported by ship over the Pacific Ocean to Balboa and then overland across the Isthmus of Panama to the Carribean Sea. Gold

---

[36] editors, 25

and silver obtained from Mexican mines also took advantage of the trade winds. The Mexican port of Veracruz was a major port for Spanish ships. In the return voyage to Spain, Spanish ships used the Gulf Stream to aid them to cross the Atlantic Ocean.

Because Spanish ships usually held gold and other treasurers, they were targets for buccaneers. The Spanish Main became a synonym for a haven for buccaneers. Spain then endeavored to challenge the buccaneers and defeat them.

Madrid, at the time, also had problems closer to home. From 1701 to 1714, Philip successfully defended his succession in the War of Spanish Succession. From 1733 to 1738, Spain supported Poland in the War of Polish Succession. From 1756 to 1763, Spain participated in the Seven Years' War, which was called the French and Indian War in America. The Treaty of Paris, which ended the war, stipulated that Spain lose Florida but gain the Louisiana territory. In 1783, at the Treaty of Versailles, Spain regained Florida from Britain, as it sided with the American colonists in the Revolution. From 1793 to 1795, Spain warred against France during the French Revolutionary Wars. Spain was defeated. In 1800, Spain ceded Louisiana territory to France. In 1808, Spain was invaded by France under Napoleon. Napoleon then named his brother, Joseph Bonaparte, as king of Spain. Spain's South American possessions used Madrid's problems as an opportunity to obtain independence. Between 1810 and 1826, the independence movement spread throughout the Spanish New World. Spain lost most of its New World possessions during this period.

During the exploration period, Spain was also burdened by two major problems that shaped its destiny and its New World possessions. One major problem was El Dragon as Francis Drake was called by his Spanish enemies. This English pirate had the blessing of the Queen of England, Elizabeth.[37]   Between Florida and Panama, Drake plundered Spanish ships and towns.   Once, he sailed through the Strait of Magellan, turned north and plundered all the Spanish towns along the South American and Mexican coasts.   When Spain sent the Armada against England, Drake was there as a vice admiral and helped defeat it.

Spain's other major problem was the Spanish Inquisition.[38]   This program was instituted by King Ferdinand and Queen Isabella when Spain was still fighting the infidel Moors in Spain.   The main purpose of the Inquisition was to root-out heretics and severely punish them.   It was well known for its barbaric cruelty and persecution. The long war with the Muslim Moor invader made religious fanatics of the Spanish people. Converting the New World Indians to the Catholic faith then became an utmost goal of Spain.   In Europe, Spain's political decisions were also greatly influenced by religion.   The Spanish Inquisition continued until early in the nineteenth century.

---

[37] Ibid., 40
[38] National Geographic Society, 177

III

Native People

Thousands of years ago, perhaps as many as 30,000 years, people crossed a land bridge from Asia to North America. From here, they settled in every part of North and South America. Some migrants may have been seafaring settlers who made their way in small boats following the North Pacific Rim and then south along the Pacific Coast of the Americas.[39] In time, they migrated from coastal areas to the interior.

Some immigrants developed advanced civilizations. The first-known civilization was established between 1200 B.C. and 400 B.C. and occupied the area between central Mexico and El Salvador. These were the Olmec people.[40] They are known for erecting large stone basalt heads, some as much as ten feet tall and many weighing 60 tons each. The heads had slanted eyes and thick lips. The Olmec disappeared about 400 B.C.

A better-known Indian civilization was the Maya, which occupied the Yucatan Peninsula. Although isolated from technical knowledge found in the Eastern Hemisphere, the Maya, nonetheless, developed comparable accomplishments. They designed mansions, pyramids, and palaces that so impressed the first Europeans that viewed them believed that the area had been colonized by ancient Egyptians. They were also able to predict eclipses, which

---

[39] Petit, 56
[40] National Geographic Society, 36

required advanced mathematical skills. Around 900 A.D., the Maya civilization collapsed for unknown reasons.

There is scientific evidence supporting the Mayan's knowledge of the orbital distance of all nine planets and solar system's asteroid belt.[41] Even more surprising was the Mayan calendar. Today's calendar reveals that the solar year is 365.2425 days, an error of 0.003 days. The Mayan calculated the solar year to be 365.2420 days, an error of 0.002 days.

Several centuries after the collapse of the Mayan culture, another civilization, the Aztec, developed in nearby central Mexico. It was described as the most brilliant and accomplished of early American civilizations. The early Aztecs took refuge on an island in Lake Texcoco.[42] Here they built a city that became their capital, Tenochtitlan. Within a hundred years, their capital became a city of temple-pyramids, palaces and great market places.

The Aztecs were extremely warlike and by military power and political deception were able to conquer all the nearby tribes. Conquered people were obligated to pay tribute to the Aztecs in gold, silver and jade. Captives were also used as a sacrifice to their gods. In one four-day ritual, 20,000 captives were sacrificed by inserting a knife beneath their ribs and ripping out their still beating hearts. The Aztecs' treatment of captives created a condition wherein they had many enemies.

Farther south in today's South America two sophisticated cultures developed in approximately present day Peru. These were the Nazca and Moche people who

---

[41] Angel, 15
[42] National Geographic Society, 144

were developing as early as 3000 B.C.[43] The most enduring legacy of the Nazca society was their geometric etchings hundreds of feet long carved in the earth. Archeologists and other scientists have yet to conclude a definite meaning to the etchings. After several centuries of existence the Nazca disappeared for reasons yet to be determined.

The Moche culture developed sometime after the disappearance of the Nazca. It reached a peak in 400 A.D. The most significant legacy of the Moche people was their skill in metal working. They developed a process of covering copper with gold. Like the Nazca, the Moche disappeared for unknown reasons.

Following on the footsteps of the Nazca and Moche cultures was the Inca civilization. It along with the Aztec civilization were the two most advanced in the New World. Both were plundered by the Spanish conquistadores. Incas or "people of the sun" probably settled in the Cuzco Valley of Peru some 300 years before the Spanish conquest, which occurred in 1532. Historical records, which were well preserved, reveled that the Inca spoke two allied languages: Amara and Quichua. However, they had no knowledge of writing. Their most lasting legacies were garden terraces cut into the sides of mountains and stone-cutting. Huge stones some 20 feet tall and weighing several tons were fitted together to form ramparts. Today, after several centuries, a knife blade cannot be placed between them.

The best example of Inca's stone-cutting ability is the citadel of Sacsayhuaman.[44] The citadel is composed of

---

[43] National Geographic Society, 84
[44] Angel, 17

huge stones, some weighing over 400 tons and cut so precisely that no mortar was used to fit the stones together. Today architects would be unable to duplicate the precision. A Spanish chronicler on the scene described the mountaintop citadel: Its proportions are inconceivable when one has not actually seen it. And when one has looked at it closely and examined it attentively, they appear to be so extraordinary that it seems as though some magic had presided over its construction—that it must be the work of demons instead of human beings. It is made of such great stones, and in such great numbers, that one wonders how the Indians were able to quarry them, how they transported them, and how they hewed them and set them one on top of the other with such precision. For they were disposed of neither iron nor steel with which to penetrate the rock and cut and polish the stones; they had neither wagon nor oxen that would have sufficed for the task, so enormous are these stones and so rude the mountain paths over which they were conveyed.

Incas rode llamas and used them as beasts of burden and a source of wool. Incas were the first to grow potatoes. Other important crops were Indian corn, sweet potatoes, and cassava. At its peak, the Inca population was believed to be between eight and ten million.

Probably the most telling influence in the development of the Eastern and Western Hemispheres was the horse. Horses were plentiful in the east, while they were totally absent in the west. Horses with their great strength and endurance can transport heavy loads. The horse gave the Eastern Hemisphere a distinct advantage in the development of their civilizations. The only trainable animals in the Western Hemisphere, except llamas in Peru, were dogs. The llama stands about five feet at the shoulder and able to carry a load of about 120 pounds. A horse on the other hand, depending upon its breed, can carry much heavier loads.

Archeologists believe that the Indian population and development of the Western Hemisphere were not evenly distributed. About the time the first Europeans came to the New World, the greatest Indian population was in South America, almost 45 million. In Mexico and Central America, the Indians' population was about 30 million. Indians north of the Rio Grande River numbered about one million.

Indians north of the Rio Grande River were not so accomplished as the Indians farther south. Most adhered to a Stone Age life. Indians east of the Mississippi River, living in woodlands, specialized in trade between tribes. They also cleared the land for farming. They became successful growing maize and beans. This became known as the Hopewell culture, which ended about 400 A.D. In turn, this was followed by the Mississippi Culture, which is noted for establishing communities with populations for as many as 30,000 people.[45]

Indians farther west, in the Great Plains, became nomads and never progressed beyond being hunters and gatherers. They became a product of their environment and adapted to it like the Indians living in the wooded areas in the east. In the Great Plains, the area was treeless, but had ample grass to feed large buffalo herds, deer and antelope.

Perhaps the most influential Indians on the American way of life were the Iroquois. The Iroquois were among

---

[45] Griffin-Pierce, 8

the first Indians encountered by the English settlers in what is now known as the East Coast of the United States.[46] They were helpful in showing the new settlers how to survive in the new and unfamiliar land. They showed them how to hunt and what wild berries were eatable. They also showed them how to grow a variety of vegetables that were unknown to them in Europe. The Iroquois grew corn, squashes, beans, and tobacco.

The first successful English settlement was at Jamestown in 1607, and, subsequently, other settlements followed. Probably, the first encounter with an Iroquois by an English settler was in the same year. The English population thrived and the colonists began to take on a new identity. In time they came to believe that London was too far away to know the problems faced by them. The settlers came to think of themselves of something more than being citizens of England. This was particularly true of new generations born in the new land. England became a distant land. Many of its laws and traditions were not applicable to their lives in the new land. The settlers developed their own traditions and ideas that were more applicable to them. Probably their interaction with the Iroquois was an integral part of their new ideas.

During the French and Indian War, 1754-1763, the Iroquois sided with the British and Americans. This decision was not out of love for the British as it was anger with the French. In 1609, French commander, Champlain, allied his forces with the Iroquois' enemy, the Algonquin Indians. With French weapons, the Algonquins successfully invaded Iroquois country. The Iroquois never

---

[46] Ibid., 24

forgot or forgave the French. Later, the Iroquois obtained modern firearms from Dutch traders and retook the territory lost to the Algonquins.

The French and Indian War drew the Iroquois and American settlers closer together, as they were allies in the war with the French. Another tangible benefit of the war was the experience gained by George Washington. Washington was a colonel in the colonial army, which was considered second rate by the British. Nonetheless, Washington could acquire first-hand experience observing British and French military tactics.

Probably the most fruitful experience gained by the colonists was their awareness of the Iroquois government. One of the Iroquois' virtues, which was surprising to the colonists, was the standing of their chiefs. Among the Iroquois, the chiefs served the people. In Europe, the people were subservient to the king.

About the time Colombus discovered America, the Iroquois tribe was divided into five nations: the Mohawk, the Oneida, the Onondaga, the Cayuga, and the Seneca. About two centuries later, the Tuscarora nation joined the other five when they were pushed out of the Carolinas by the English settlers. These Iroquois nations had been constantly at war with one another until Deganawidah, a Huron prophet, was inspired to create a unified government and the Great Peace.

Deganawidah had a vision of a great spruce tree that touched the sky and had five roots, representing the five nations. He envisioned this a spiritual tree of peace and unity that encompassed three human principles for living: health of body and sanity of mind; righteousness in thought, speech, and behavior, and sufficient civil authority and strength. At first, representatives of the five nations rejected the Great Peace, as they did not want to give up their freedom and independence. About 1600, after careful deliberation, the five nations accepted the plan that evolved into a strong confederacy, which became known as The League of the Iroquois. In 1722, the Tuscarora joined the Iroquois Confederacy.

The Iroquois political system was distinctive and quite different from anything the settlers had known. The system was based upon clan membership. Each tribe was composed of three to eight clans. Each clan was represented by male chiefs and when combined with other chiefs in the tribe, it became the chief's council. The combined chiefs' council of all the tribes formed the league council. The league council held veto power over decisions made by the tribes.

Each tribe also had its women's council, which was chosen from the mothers in the tribe. As mothers of warriors, the women's council decided questions of war and peace. The council also took initiatives in resolving problems affecting the tribe. Their most significant role was in nominating members to the chief's council. In some ways, the Iroquois government paralleled the existing American government. The women's council was equivalent to the American legislative branch and the league council equivalent to the executive branch.

The English colonists were directly influenced by The League of the Iroquois. In 1754, some colonists wanted to draft a plan of unity among the American colonies. It was to be called the Albany Plan of Union. Naturally many colonies did not want to lose their autonomy. Benjamin Franklin reminded the colonists, "It would be a strange thing if the six nations of the Iroquois should be capable of forming and executing a scheme for such a union…and yet that a like union should be impractical for ten or a dozen English colonies, to whom it is more necessary…"[47]

Later, when the English colonists decided upon a path of independence, they would draw upon their experience with the Iroquois and new European thought known as "The Age of Enlightenment." In the eighteenth century, Paris became the center of enlightened thought. In 1690, John Locke, an English philosopher, wrote that people have natural rights to life, liberty, and property and they have a contract with their government to achieve these ends. Locke's ideas inspired other European philosophers to broaden his concepts. French philosophers, Voltaire or Jean Francois-Marie Arouet, and Charles Louis De Secondat Montesquieu were the principal architects of "The Age of Enlightenment." Montesquieu was particularly important to the English colonists. He wrote *The Spirit of the Laws* that described a government divided into three branches: legislative, executive, and judicial.

These philosophers gave the English colonists a new perspective of government. Lofty, theoretical ideals, though, are not always practical. The English colonists, however, could draw upon their knowledge of The League of the Iroquois for a practical view of a democratic form of government. The English colonists had interacted with the Iroquois for more than a century and half before declaring their independence. At the outbreak of hostilities with the British, the Iroquois, themselves, recommended their political system for the American dissidents. After

---

[47] Ibid., 32

independence, some colonists, though, were still uncertain about a democratic government. They asked that George Washington be king. Fortunately, Washington rejected this notion out of hand.

IV

Horse Indians

Early native American Indian tribes in Texas were the Caddo, Tonkawa, Atakapa, and Karankawa. Later the Apaches, Comanches and Wichitas moved into Texas. Most Indian groups occupied Texas in a transitory state. There is evidence that at least twelve tribes lived in Texas from time to time. The most dominant tribe, though, was the Comanche. No other tribe had such a lasting impact on the history of Texas as the Comanche.

Originally, the Comanches were a mountain people and a part of the Shoshonean family of tribes, which included the Shoshone, Ute, Bannock, and several other Rocky Mountain tribes. These tribes occupied the country between the Yellowstone and Platt Rivers in what is now Wyoming.

Early in the eighteenth century, the Comanches left their Rocky Mountain home and moved to the South Plains. They proceeded to occupy the country south of the Arkansas River, which the Comanches called the Flint Arrow Point River. It is generally accepted that the Comanche was the only division of the Shoshonean family to live entirely on the plains.

In 1705, the Comanches in company with some Utes appeared in New Mexico. The Comanches asked for peace, but as they left, they stole horses. This was probably the beginning of one of the most monumental happenings in American history. The horse, the Plains and the

33

Comanches, when united into a single force, produced a barrier to all encroaching people: Spanish, French, English, Mexican, Texan, and American.

South of the Arkansas River the Comanches occupied an area of about 24,000 square miles. This area encompassed Southeastern Colorado, Southwestern Kansas, Western Oklahoma, Eastern New Mexico, and most of West Texas. Although, the Comanche's territory included five states as delineated on today's maps, the maps of the 19th century did show that the Comanche's territory was all in Texas. It was not until 1850, after the Mexican War, did Texas and other Western states obtain their present boundaries. Historians estimate that about 20,000 Comanches occupied this vast area by the mid eighteenth century.[48]

The Comanches had an unusual method of governing their people. It was probably incomparable. Moreover, it was probably the best method of governing the vast Comanche territory. The Comanche people were held together by tradition and a code that they voluntarily subscribed to. Had they not voluntarily submitted to the code, there would probably be no trace of the Comanche today. Archeologists would only note that at one time an unknown, transitory group of people passed through this area.

The Comanches had no single chief or central authority controlling the tribe. The Comanche tribe was divided into five or more divisions. Frequently, small bands would form out of one division. Each band was independent and the divisions were autonomous.

---

[48] Rollings, 24

Bands were usually formed from a family or a group of families. If they desired, they could move from one Comanche division to another or remain independent. They had a common culture and intermarriage between divisions was common. Ten Bears, a Yamparika Comanche leader, proclaimed the meaning of the Comanche's life:[49]

I was born upon the prairie, where the wind blew free and there was nothing to break the light of the sun. I was born where there were no enclosures and where everything drew a fresh breath. I want to die there and not remain within walls. I know every stream and every wood between the Rio Grande and the Arkansas. I have hunted and lived over that country. I live like my fathers before me and like them I lived happily.

There were only three sources of power in the tribe,[50] and they were severely limited. The Comanches had a peace chief, band council, and a war chief. The peace chief was usually an older man in the band. He could only advise or suggest. When several bands combined, the peace chiefs in each band would recognize, by general consent, one of their number to be peace chief of the combined bands. He remained peace chief only as long as the bands stayed together. The other band chiefs advised the overall peace chief.

---

[49] Ibid., 83
[50] Ibid., 26

The duty of the peace chief was to act as mediator and keep peace within the band. His efforts were limited to his band's internal affairs. If people stopped listening to his advice, he lost his position as peace chief.

The band council decided upon more significant actions. It decided where and when the band should move, caring for the weak and elderly, war or peace, and trade with outsiders. The band council consisted of all adult men. The younger men usually kept silent and left most of the decisions to the more mature men. Women were permitted to listen to the proceeding but usually did not participate. Occasionally, men asked for the opinions of women who responded with a dignified demeanor.

The decisions arrived at by the band council had to be unanimous. If unanimity was not obtained, the band council would postpone a decision. The Comanches believed unanimity was essential to preserve harmony and unity within the band. If general unanimity could not be reached, the dissentient group would leave the band and probably form a new band. They would, however, remain Comanche.

One duty of the band council was to choose a war chief. Usually the war chief was selected from recognized successful warriors and had the respect of other warriors. Once selected, a war chief had only limited authority. In battle, all warriors willingly followed the orders of the war chief. When the war party returned to camp, the war chief lost his authority. He was treated no differently from any other warrior in camp.

Robert S. Neighbors, U.S. appointed special agent for Indians in Texas in 1847, described the proceedings of a

Comanche council:[51] The subjects under discussion in the council are always open to popular opinion, and the chiefs are the main exponents of it. The democratic principle is strongly implanted in them. They consult, principally, the warrior class, and the weaker minds are wholly influenced by popular opinion. Each man endeavors to obtain as high a position as their merits allow. War chiefs commit hostilities without consulting the other tribes. Any proposition or treaties proposed by the whites are discussed privately, and the answer given by the chief as the unanimous voice of the tribe. In deliberations in the council, they consult each other, and one addresses the meeting. The council is opened by passing the council pipe from one to the other, and invoking the Deity to preside. It is conducted with great propriety and closed in the same manner. There is one appointed as crier or messenger, whose duty it is to fill the pipe...

During a major war campaign the bands probably joined a division to obtain greater strength. The Spaniards and Americans identified 13 regional Comanche divisions in the eighteenth and nineteenth centuries. However, five major divisions were the generally accepted number of readily identifiable Comanche divisions.

The Penateka Comanches were the southernmost division.[52] Their name means honey-eaters because they could acquire honey in the trees that were found in their region. They occupied the area between the Edwards Plateau and the Cross Timbers.

---

[51] Richardson, 11
[52] Rollins, 23

The division just north of the area occupied by the Penateka Comanches was the Nokoni Comanches who later changed their name to Detsanayuka. Their name means: those who turn back or wanderers. Grouped with this division were the Tenawa and Tanima bands. Together they were known as the Middle Comanches.

North of the Middle Comanches were the Kotsoteka Comanches or Buffalo Eaters. The main diet of all Comanches was buffalo meat, but the Kotsoteka occupied the area between the Red River and the Canadian River where buffalo herds were always found.

North of the Kotsoteka Comanches were the Yamparika Comanches or root eaters. They retained the Shoshone habit of eating the roots of the yampa vine. They occupied the area between the Canadian and Arkansas Rivers.

The fifth Comanche division was the Quahadi Comanche or antelopes. They were also known as the western Comanches. They occupied the area known as the Llano Estacado or staked plains, which is in the northwestern part of Texas and extends into eastern New Mexico.

The word Comanche was little known among the Comanches. The Comanches called themselves Nimma, which translates: the people.[53] The French called them Padoucas, while the Spanish called them Komantcia. The Ute Indians called them Kwumaci, which means stranger. As the Spanish were only able to communicate with the Utes, they probably adopted the Ute name for the Comanches with some variation. The Americans adopted the Spanish name with another variation.

---

[53] Richardson, 2

The physical appearance of the Comanches varied by two eyewitness accounts. George Catlin, an artist and western explorer who accompanied the Dragoon Expedition of 1834 to Comanche country, described the Comanches, "...short, heavy, and ungainly in their movements, all in all a most unattractive and slovenly looking race of Indians."[54]

Texas pioneer, John H. Jenkins, described the Comanches: "The warriors were almost without exception large, fine-looking men, displaying to the very best advantage their erect, graceful, well-knit frames and finely proportioned figures, being entirely naked, with the exception of a small apron attached to a belt or girdle, which was made of cloth of all textures and colors, with fringes and tassels at the ends. They had keen black eyes without lashes, and long plaits of coarse black hair hanging from their bare heads down the very ground behind them."

The Comanches' primary diet was protein from buffalo meat. Nutritionists have concluded that meat obtained from buffalo is lower in fat than meat from beef cattle. Also, the Comanches spent most of their time on horseback, which is something of an athletic activity. The combination of the two, a high protein diet coupled with an athletic activity, probably produced a lean, muscular man.

George Catlin described Comanche horsemanship in 1834: "I am ready without hesitation to pronounce the Comanches the most extraordinary horsemen that I have seen yet in all my travels, and I doubt very much whether any people in the world can surpass them. A Comanche on his feet is out of his element, and comparatively almost as

---

[54] Newcomb, 158

awkward as a monkey on the ground, without a limb or branch to cling to; but the moment he lays his hands upon his horse his face even becomes handsome, and he gracefully flies away like a different being."[55]

Horses dominated the life of a Comanche. The Comanche went everywhere on a horse. He was never without his horse. The horse vastly increased his efficiency in hunting buffalo, his principal source of food, clothing, weapons, and shelter. It was the principal reason the Comanche was called a Horse Indian. It was common for a Comanche to possess 250 horses. Some more important warriors owned as many as a thousand.[56]

Horse ownership was a mark of wealth and prestige. The greater the number, the greater the wealth and prestige. Horses were also mediums of exchange and, more importantly, they increased the mobility of the Comanches. It was practical to own a large remuda to endure the rigors of a long range raid. It was not uncommon for a Comanche raid to extend to over 600 miles. A Comanche warrior could easily travel 70 miles a day on horseback. After some distance, say 15 miles, depending upon the terrain and other like factors, a Comanche simply changed to a fresh horse. By contrast, U.S. cavalrymen rode 25 miles on a good day. On a forced march, they could ride for about 65 miles in two days, but this increased rate could not be endured without a long rest period.[57]

Many Comanche horsemanship qualities were copied from their unwilling Spanish mentors. They mounted their

---

[55] Capps, 55
[56] Rollings, 34
[57] Nevin, *The Soldiers*, 109

horses from the right side as did the Spanish,[58] whose habit had been acquired from the Moor invader. In other ways they improved upon the Spanish methods.

Spaniards rode only stallions,[59] which sometimes bucked when under stress. The Comanches gelded most of their male horses. A gelding was more easily trainable and, thus, made into a war or buffalo horse. Such a horse had to respond to a rider's commands transmitted through his knees or through a shift in his body weight.

In 1835, the artist, George Catlin, wrote of Comanche horsemanship: "Among their feats of riding, one astonished me... Every young man...is able to drop his body upon the side of his horse...effectually screened from his enemies' weapons as he lays in a horizontal position...with his heel hanging over the horse's back; by which he has the power of throwing himself up again, and changing to the other side of the horse if necessary... He will hang whilst his horse is at fullest speed, carrying with him his bow and his shield, and also his long lance."[60]

A Comanche warrior would never ride a mare in battle or on a hunt. Mares were generally reserved for women and children. A swayback horse was used to carry a pack or pull a travois, which was the Indian's version of a trailer.[61] It consisted of two long shafts tied together near the horse's head and widened behind the horse where the two shafts were rigidly fitted together by a smaller shaft. The two long shafts then extended rearward where they dragged the ground.

---

[58] Newcomb, 90
[59] Capps, 60
[60] Rollings, 42
[61] Capps, 57

J. Frank Dobie, a Texas author, paid the Comanches a tribute: "Their essence survived on the arid borders of Texas where the saying was common: A white man will ride the mustang until he is played out; a Mexican will take him and ride him another day until he thinks he is played out; then a Comanche will mount him, and ride him to where he is going."[62]

A Comanche always owned one or two favorite horses. These were kept near his lodge at night for safety's sake. Post Oak Jim, a Comanche, said, "Some men loved their horses more than their wives."[63] When horse thieves from other tribes were in the area, the favorite horse was brought into the Comanche's tepee, which then forced the wife to sleep outside.[64]

The acquisition of horses was the principal reason for Comanche raids.[65] Stealing horses was their preferred method of acquisition.[66] Their enemies, principally Apaches and Spaniards, were prime targets for horse thievery. Colonel Richard I. Dodge, when he was at Fort Chadbourne in Texas, said of the Comanches: "Where all are such magnificent thieves, it is difficult to decide which of the Plains tribes deserves the palm for stealing. The Indians themselves give it to the Comanches, whose designation in the sign language is a backward, wriggling motion of the index finger, signifying a snake, and indicating the silent stealth of that tribe. For crawling into a camp, cutting hopples and lariat ropes, and getting off

---

[62] Newcomb, 88
[63] Capps, 61
[64] Ibid., 67
[65] Newcomb, 184
[66] Capps, 184

undiscovered with the animals, they are unsurpassed and unsurpassable."[67]

Another observer of the Plains said, "A Comanche could crawl into a bivouac where a dozen men where sleeping, each with a horse tied to his wrist by the lariat, cut a rope within six feet of the sleeper, and get away with the horse without waking a soul."[68] A Comanche, however, would never steal from a friend or another Comanche. Strangers and enemies, though, were fair game.

The Comanches were also well adapted at capturing wild horses.[69] Their favorite method was to build a corral near a watering hole. They used trees and brush to form the walls of the corral, which was open at only one end. From the opening two arms of high brush extended outward several hundred yards. The two arms were narrow at the corral entrance and wide at the end of the extended arms. The two arms were like a large funnel in which the Comanches drove the horses into the coral.

The Comanches hid themselves near the watering hole. After some horses came to the watering hole and drank their fill of water, the Comanches came out of hiding and rushed among the slow-moving, water logged animals. The Comanches then surrounded the wild horses and drove them toward their corral where they were easily roped.

The Comanches also hunted wild horses in winter when grass was scarce and, thus, the animals were weaker. Cold weather and lack of food made the horses an easy catch for

---

[67] Newcomb, 155
[68] Capps, 54
[69] Rollings, 32

the Comanches. Therefore, the Comanches usually did not need to construct corrals in winter to capture wild horses.

The principal reason for possessing horses was to secure more horses and to hunt buffalo. Professor W.W. Newcomb best described the Comanche's relationship with the horse and buffalo: "If the horse is thought of as the vehicle which bore the cultures of the Plains Indians, then the buffalo becomes the fuel which propelled it."[70]

On a typical hunt, the Comanches chose a responsible hunt leader who served as hunt director and coordinator.[71] The other Comanches on the hunt willingly followed the hunt leader's instructions. When a buffalo herd was located, the Comanches approached it from the downwind side and slowly encircled it, leaving the upwind side open until last. The Comanches then tightened the circle until the buffalo came in range of their arrows. The Comanches, while on horseback, approached a buffalo from the right side and loosed an arrow behind the last rib to penetrate the animal's diaphragm and thereby collapse its lungs. Sometimes the Comanches used their lances to strike the buffalo in the same area. The Comanches preferred to use their primitive weapons on a hunt even after they obtained firearms.

When a buffalo was killed, every portion of its body was utilized by the Comanches.[72] Most of the buffalo was converted to food. Other body parts, though, were put to good use. The tongue was a source of food and a hairbrush. The skull was used in ceremonies. The horns

---

[70] Newcomb, 90

[71] Ibid., 162

[72] Griffin-Pierce, 74

were made into spoons, ladles, and headdresses. Muscles and sinew were used to make bows and thread. The hair was used to make pillows, rope, halters and bridles. The bones were converted into knives, arrowheads, and splints. The paunch was made into cooking vessels. The hooves were made into rattles and glue. Even the dung was used as fuel. The hide was converted to moccasins, bedding, clothing, and tepee lining. To make a tepee, twelve to sixteen feet in diameter, required about ten buffalo hides.[73]

The Comanches were always frugal when taking buffalo. They only killed what they needed for food and then used all parts of its body. They never engaged in wanton slaughter of buffalos. This was even more apparent after the Comanches acquired horses. After possessing horses, they no longer needed to stampede buffalos over a cliff. A Comanche on horseback could kill buffalos one at a time to satisfy his needs. On the other hand, a buffalo stampede could, at times, kill more buffalos than could be consumed.

After a buffalo hunt, all the meat could not be consumed at the kill site. The Comanches, thus, devised a method of preserving meat. A former Comanche captive described this process:

> They would make a kind of box out of rawhide, two or three feet long, and about twenty inches wide, so it will fit a packsaddle. They cut the meat thin and hang it up to dry and when packing they fold the dry sheets of meat and put it in these rawhide boxes and place a box on each side of the

---

[73] Ibid. 77

packsaddle, and carry it with them. Many is the time I have slyly loosened the string on a box and swiped some of the dried meat. It was real good, and very palatable the way the Indians prepared it.[74]

Probably the Comanches believed that the buffalo existed in limitless numbers. When Europeans first entered North America, they described the buffalo herds as "tremendous tidal waves whose extent and number stagger the imagination."[75]   No one knows with certainty the number of buffalo that existed in North America. Scholars, however, estimate the number at 60 million when Europeans first arrived.[76]   Most of the buffalo were concentrated in the Great Plains north of Mexico.

The Great Plains today is quite different from the time of the Comanches. Formerly, the Great Plains had a thin top soil but was adequate to support the growth of a thick, rich grass that provided food for buffalo, elk, deer, and antelope.[77] Subsequently, Spanish horses found the plains equally supportive.

The Plains of today would probably be a desert if it were not for man-made irrigation. One reason given for the cause of the destruction of the Plains was over cultivation. During World War I, there was a great demand for wheat. Consequently, the thin top soil of the Plains was destroyed by plowing to satisfy the demand for wheat, and then wind did the rest to create a dust bowl.

---

[74] Richardson, 9
[75] Newcomb, 91
[76] Rollings, 34
[77] Ibid., 22

The Comanches readily adapted to life on the Plains. The transition from mountain life to life on the plains was simplified by a favorable environment. The dry and relatively flat land was crossed by several large rivers that flowed from the northwest to the southeast. These rivers, which were wide and shallow, were the Cimarron, Canadian, Washita, Red, Pease, Brazos, and Pecos. Most were about 100 yards wide and about one yard deep.[78] The rivers were usually lined with cottonwood, elm, walnut, pecan, and persimmon trees. The rivers provided water and the trees provided shelter and food.[79] The Comanches also collected wild-plant products found on the plains. These included plums, grapes, currants, juniper berries, mulberries, persimmons, tunas of the prickly pear, and pemmican. Berries and nuts were generally used to flavor the dried buffalo meat.[80]

Although meat was the principal food of the Comanches, they did eat fruits and vegetables whenever they could be found.[81] Prickly pears grown by cactus were eaten when available. A certain root, something like a wild potato, was in particular demand. The Comanches also perfected a method of making bread from mesquite tree beans.

The Comanches also had certain food fetishes.[82] They would not eat birds, fish, dogs, coyotes, or pork. Pork in particular was deemed unclean. Eating a dog was like

---

[78] Ibid., 21
[79] Ibid., 22
[80] Newcomb, 163
[81] Richardson, 9
[82] Ibid. 9 & Newcomb, 163

eating one's own grandmother.[83] Also, they would not eat food broiled and boiled on the same fire. A separate fire was required for the broiled food and another fire for the boiled food.[84]

The Comanches prescribed to a noteworthy moral code. In general, they were regarded to have a higher moral code than other Plains Indians.[85] This concept is surprising to most Americans and Europeans, as they believed that all Indians were savages. The Comanches, however, were hospitable and would share their last bit of food with a guest. They were fearless in battle but would not torture hapless enemies. Nevertheless, a defeated enemy was treated harshly. A Comanche warrior, though, did not expect mercy if he were captured. Thus, most battles ended without taking prisoners.

The Comanches were also compassionate. Clinton Smith, a former boy captive, related his experience traveling with a Comanche band:[86] when water was not found at a certain place where it was expected, the most rigid discipline was enforced in the interest of the weaker members of the band. Grim warriors, with bloodshot eyes and swollen tongues, staggered on, threatening with death anyone who might attempt to drink the few cupfuls of water carried in buffalo paunches and doled out to the little children.

Children were highly prized among the Comanches.[87] The tribe had a low birth rate and death at child birth was

---

[83] Capps, 32

[84] Newcomb, 163

[85] Richardson, 17

[86] Ibid., 9

[87] Newcomb, 166

not unusual.   Although children of either sex were welcomed and loved, boy babies were particularly valued. Boys would eventually become warriors whose duty was to provide meat and protect the home.

Though children were particularly welcomed, the Comanches had a harsh custom when dealing with defective or abnormal babies.[88] They were abandoned and left to die.   The abandonment measure also applied to twins, particularly if they were girls. With boys, only one twin was abandoned.

The age at which a boy became a warrior was not exact.[89] He first had to participate in a major buffalo hunt, which was preceded by a hunt of lesser animals such as deer and antelope. The second step, which was expressly meaningful to Comanches, was to receive a visionary quest. Once received, the boy was then spiritually guided and protected by a supernatural guardian. The boy was then qualified to join a war party. If he showed promise on a raid, he was then regarded as a warrior. He was eligible to marry and receive other benefits accorded to his new status.

Marriage among Comanches was a simple procedure. If a man wanted a certain girl for his wife, he presented the girl's parents with a gift, usually a horse or horses. If his suit was accepted, the horses were driven into the coral with the other horses owned by the girl's parents.   The suitor then took his bride to his tepee.[90]

Marriage among Comanches may appear somewhat cut and dry. There was, however, a courtship period preceding

---

[88] Ibid., 166
[89] Ibid., 168
[90] Ibid., 169

the marriage.[91]   The Comanche's custom was that young boys and girls could not be seen together in public. Therefore, enterprising youths devised schemes to overcome this obstacle, which added to the excitement of the moment. When girls went for water, they were often intercepted by their suitors.   After becoming better acquainted, a boy may sneak into the girl's tepee at night and ask her to slip away with him.

Generally, polygyny was not practiced by the Comanches, as the number of women and men were about equal. However, when a man married a certain girl, he was expected to inherit his wife's younger sisters who automatically became additional wives. This arrangement was welcomed by the wife, as her sisters could assist her in the many burdensome duties.   Also, if the man had a brother, it was the custom for him to share his wife with his brother, especially if one brother was away on a raid. If the brother were killed, then the surviving brother married his brother's widow.[92]   This custom provided family stability and tribal unity.   The new wife treated children from another wife as her own.

Hunting and going to war was the principal occupation of the Comanches.   It was the only reason for being a Comanche.   A visiting German scientist, Dr. Ferdinand Roemer, witnessed a Comanche war party preparing for a raid into Mexico.   He observed that the warriors painted their faces red and most wore a buffalo headdress.   Their shields, made of buffalo leather, were painted with gaudy

---

[91] Ibid., 169
[92] Ibid., 170

colors and decorated with feathers. Their horses' heads and tails were also painted red.

The material for their weapons of war, bows and arrows, was selected with great care. The most sought after wood for a bow was from the *Bois d'arc* tree, which incidentally shows the French influence on Indian culture. *Bois d'arc* translated from French means wood for the bow.[93] It is also known as the Osage orange tree. It was the duty of the older men in the tribe, those that could no longer go to war, to make the bows. Wood for the bows was selected from green trees and cut into four foot lengths. The cut wood was then moved to the camp site where it was scraped and shaved to three foot lengths.[94] The wood was then allowed to dry, which may have required several months. Afterwards, the wood was whittled to its final shape and then greased with animal fat. Sinew from buffalo tendons covered with glue obtained from boiled hooves was then wrapped around the wood.

Once the decision was made to go to war or make a raid, a war leader was chosen. Warriors had the option of following the war leader or not. A war leader who had been successful in previous raids would have little difficulty in recruiting others to follow him. On the other hand, an inexperienced leader may not recruit any followers. Warriors who agreed to follow a certain leader imposed a discipline upon themselves to follow all orders of the war leader.[95]

---

[93] Rollings, 35
[94] Ibid., 35
[95] Newcomb, 182

Whether going to war or making a raid, the Comanches never passed an opportunity to steal horses. Their favorite tactic was to strike swiftly, take loot, and then quickly withdraw.[96] If the enemy were not surprised, they would attempt to lay an ambush. Another tactic used, when the enemy was not surprised, was to try to encircle him. This tactic was a favorite when the enemy was fewer in number. In a battle with the Comanches, one defender observed this tactic first hand:

> It was a strange spectacle never to be forgotten, the wild, fantastic band as they stood in battle array, or swept around us with all strategy of Indian warfare. Twenty or thirty warriors, mounted upon splendid horses, tried to ride around us, sixty or eighty yards distant, firing upon us as they went. It was a superstition among them, that if they could thus run around a force they could certainly vanquish it.[97]

The Comanches practiced scalping, which was considered savagery by Europeans and Americans. For the Comanche, this was visible proof of victory over an enemy.[98] Also, scalping an enemy prevented him from becoming immortal and returning again in a later life to strike the Comanches.[99] This Comanche practice was not much unlike the warriors under Genghis Khan whose vast hoards conquered Korea, China, Russia and Persia in the

---

[96] Ibid., 183
[97] Ibid., 183
[98] Rollings, 47
[99] Newcomb, 189

thirteenth century. The Khan's warriors cut the ears off fallen enemy warriors and tossed them into sacks. Later, the ears were brought to camp where they were counted at leisure.

Injuries such as broken bones and gunshot wounds were to be expected of a Comanche warrior-hunter. Medicine men, though, developed crude but effective techniques to overcome these injuries.[100] They knew the benefits of a tourniquet, used various beneficial herbs, and did some limited surgery. They also devised several effective cures for rattlesnake bites.[101] Also to arrest inflamation, they made a compound of prickly pear leaves applied to the infected area. To cure tuberculosis, the Comanches used the plant: black nightshades.[102] As an overall cure, the Comanches devised a steam bath oven constructed with bogs and covered with skins. Hot stones were placed in the center and sprinkled with water. A dense vapor was produced that induced the patient to sweat profusely. Afterwards, the patient was encouraged to jump into a cold stream.

Being nomads, the Comanches frequently moved their campsite. When the Comanches moved an encampment, an unforgettable sight was brought forward.[103] The German scientist, Dr. Roemer, expressed his admiration:

> According to Indian custom they rode a single file, the men in advance, dressed in their best, looking about, dignified and grave; the lively

---

[100] Ibid, 187
[101] Richardson, 15
[102] Capps., 139
[103] Newcomb, 165

squaws following, sitting astride like the men, each usually carrying a black-eyed little papoose on her back and another in front of the saddle. Simultaneously they kept a watchful eye on the pack horse which carried the skins and the various household goods.

Frequently changing campsites was the accepted life of the Comanches. They readily adapted to this life and developed their own instinctive guidelines when on the trail. If the Comanches were tracked by an enemy, and it was not advantageous to fight, the Comanches used an effective ruse. They scattered skunk musk on the trail to deaden their scent.[104] They also used various methods of concealing their movements by observing and then duplicating wild animals. The wolf was held as a brother and often warned of danger. If a wolf appeared before them on the trail, the Comanches would change course or stop for the day.[105] A horned toad was believed to run in the direction of buffalo. If a raven circled over a Comanche camp and cawed, it would then fly in the direction of buffalo.[106]

---

[104] Richardson, 13
[105] Ibid., 14
[106] Capps, 127

V

The Comancheria

The Comanches, as with most Indians north of the Rio Grande, believed that they were part of nature and not separate from it. Indeed, they were elements of the earth. The term, "Mother Earth," had a literal meaning to the American Indians. "We are made from the Earth, My Mother,"[107] said George Blueeyes, a Navajo Elder. One cannot own his mother, and, therefore, no one can divide her. The Indians could never understand the Europeans and Americans who built fences to define their property, as no one could own the earth.

Tecumseh, a Shawnee chief said it best, "A man could no more own the land than he could the sea or the air he breathes."[108]

Like a wolf or some other predatory animal, the Comanches delineated their 24,000 square mile hunting ground.[109] This ground became known as the Comancheria or the land of the Comanches. The Comanches dominated the Comancheria and used it as a base to raid areas hundreds of miles outside their Comancheria, mostly south and west of the Rio Grande.[110] Their Indian enemies, the Apaches, Tonkawas, Pawnees and Osage felt the fury of the Comanches.

---

[107] Griffin-Pierce, 9
[108] Ibid., 30
[109] Rollings, 29
[110] Richardson, 31

The Apache, a powerful Indian tribe, migrated to the South Plains from Canada several centuries before the arrival of the Comanches.[111] One European traveler said of the Apache, "One of the toughest human organisms the world has ever seen." The Comanches, as proof of their might, drove the Apaches from Texas to the mountains of New Mexico.

Although the southern limit of the Comancheria was somewhat north of San Antonio, Texas, it did not save San Antonio from Comanche raids. They often raided San Antonio and settlements along the Rio Grande and then across it into Mexico.[112] An account of raids on the settlements along the Rio Grande in 1824: They were ghost towns, and little remained of the original communities, "where widows and orphans weep for dear ones slain and sons and daughters carried into captivity by these savages to villages that are over two hundred leagues away, where Christian girls are married to these barbarous people and some sold as slaves to other peoples more remote."

In 1825, there were only 59 soldiers in Texas.[113] For such a vast area as Texas, this small number of soldiers meant that Texas was unguarded. This was particularly egregious, since marauding Indians were known to be in the area.

On July 5, 1825, a band of Comanches raided San Antonio.[114] The band consisted of 226 warriors, 104 women and 44 children. They remained six days and took whatever they pleased. They entered homes, "insulting and

---

[111] Newcomb, 104
[112] Richardson, 31
[113] Richardson, 31
[114] Richardson, 31

threatening the owners with arms if they did not acquiesce or if they did not permit the Indians to take whatever they desired."

Spanish power in the New World waned at the time Comanche power waxed. Spain successfully used the horse in conquering the Aztec, Inca, and Mayan Empires. The Comanches used these same Spanish horses to neutralize Spanish attempts to conquer the Comancheria.

Spain's vast empire in the New World was more than it could govern adequately. Its empire extended from the Strait of Magellan in the south to Canada in the north. Spain did not have a surplus population to settle its New World domain. At the time, Spanish emigres to the New World numbered about 1,000 per year.[115] Most detrimental to its empire building effort was the caste system that the Spaniards brought with them to the New World. In New Spain, as Mexico was called, the Spanish emigres developed a four-tier caste system.[116] At the top of the social-political system were the Spanish emigres born in Spain. They were called *gachupines* or wearer of spurs. Second down on the tier were the Creoles, Spaniards born in the New World. Next down on the tier were the mestizos, people of mixed blood: Spanish-Indian, Spanish-Negro, and Indian-Negro. On the bottom tier were the pure-blood Indians who made up about half the population.

Spain and ultimately its New World progeny missed two philosophical experiences that were fundamental to Western Europe and the United States: The Age of

---

[115] Editors, 18
[116] Johnson, 46

Enlightenment and the Renaissance.[117] The philosophical thoughts gleaned from them were basic in the creation of the American Declaration of Independence and Constitution. Spain's life and death struggle with the Moor invader out of Africa closed Spain's perspective to new philosophical concepts being advanced at the time. American historian, Will Durant, observed, "Spain's mountains, particularly the Pyrenees were her protection and tragedy; they gave her comparative security from external attack but hindered her economic advance, her political unity, and her participation in European thought." Hence the European adage, "Africa begins at the Pyrenees."[118] Greed, superstition, hatred and fear that were part of the Spanish system live on in Mexico to this day.[119]

The Moors evolved from two North African peoples: Arab and Berber. They became Islam zealots who invaded Spain in 711. They were led by ibn Ziyad and overran all of Spain and Portugal and then crossed into France. Here they were defeated at the Battle of Poitiers by a Christian army under Charles Martel in 732. The Moors then retreated back into Spain and held it until they were driven out by the combined armies of Ferdinand and Isabella in 1492.[120]

Three centuries after the last Moor was driven from Spain, Moorish culture still held a tight grip on Spain and people in the New World. During the Battle of the Alamo in 1836, Santa Anna, the commander of the Mexican forces, ordered his band to sound *The Deguello*. *The*

---

[117] Thomas, Introduction.
[118] Thomas, 9
[119] Johnson, 43
[120] Comptons, Moors

Deguello was a Moorish march meaning throat-cutting or no quarter.

Since the Indians were held in such low esteem, the Spaniards developed the *encomienda* or entrustment system.[121] Spanish soldiers were rewarded with land grants and *encomiendas* of Indians. A deed of *encomienda* read: "Unto you are given in trust for you to make use of in your farms and mines; and you are to teach them the things of the holy Catholic faith." This system was merely a grant for free labor or slavery.

The Spanish record, though, was not all evil. A Dominican Bishop of Chiapas, Mexico, Bartolome de las Casas, believed the Indians were human and had souls.[122] This was a radical idea that earned him the hatred of all Spaniards in Mexico. A few other missionaries had ideas similar to the Bishop of Chiapas.

Spain, however, had no intention of ruining a good thing. Its holdings in the New World would only be a source of wealth for Spain. Except learning the Catholic faith, the Indians were to remain ignorant and at the bottom of the social-political order.

This idea was totally unacceptable to the Comanches. They were nomadic people and could never be tied to a mine or a hacienda. In a short time, therefore, Spain and the Comanches became rivals for the control of Texas. Although, the Comancheria covered West Texas and eastern New Mexico, Spain was unable to colonize East Texas and in no account could it colonize West Texas. The Comanches controlled the land bridge between Mexico and

---

[121] Johnson, 44
[122] Johnson, 45

East Texas. As a result, the entire eastern part of Texas lay unoccupied.[123]

A showdown between the Comanches and the Spaniards was not long in coming. Early in the 18th century, the Comanches arrived in the Comancheria and found it occupied by Apache Indians. The Comanches then began to drive the Apaches south and west of the Rio Grande River. As a defensive measure, the Apaches then hit upon an old stratagem: pit one enemy against another. Here: Comanches against Spaniards.

In 1749, a delegation of Lipan Apaches entered a Franciscan mission in San Antonio. They requested that a mission be established in their country. At the time, a mission always accompanied a presidio or garrison of soldiers. The Franciscans were overjoyed and decided to establish a mission on the San Saba River near the present town of Menard.[124] After the completion of the mission, the Franciscans were surprised by the attitude of the Apaches. The Apaches accepted gifts but refused to become converts. Only later did the Franciscans realize the intentions of the Apaches.

The Comanches concluded exactly what the Apaches expected. By establishing a mission in the Comancheria, Spain must be allied with their Apache enemies. In 1758, therefore, some 2,000 Comanches attacked the San Saba mission and destroyed it. Spain then realized that these barbarous Indians must be punished and the deaths of two missionaries, Fray Terreros and Fray Santiesteban,

---

[123] Editors, 93
[124] Ibid., 63

avenged. Most importantly, the Spanish crown must gain satisfaction.

In 1759, Spain mounted a punitive force of 600 men and two field guns to teach the Comanches a lesson. The force was assembled in San Antonio and marched north. After some time, it found several thousand Comanches and their Wichita allies behind fortifications along the Red River. Although outnumbered, the Spaniards believed they held the advantage. After all, Cortes conquered the Aztecs with about the same number of men. Cortes, though, faced an enemy without horses and firearms. This time, the Spaniards faced an enemy with Spanish horses and French firearms obtained from French traders.

The Spanish defeat was complete. They lost their two field guns and baggage train. They were forced to fall back to the San Saba River in a rout. This was the worst defeat the Spanish suffered in the New World.[125] Spain then reappraised its Hispanicization of Texas. In Texas they realized their methods did not work. Spain was forced to acknowledge that the Comanches were the real masters of Texas and never again tried to force the Comanches to do their will in Texas.[126]

The Spanish defeat at Red River had similar ramifications as the Roman defeat by German tribesman at the battle of Teutoburger Wald in AD 9.[127] Here, the Romans lost three legions, which far outweighs the defeat of only 600 Spanish soldiers. Nevertheless, the consequences of the defeats were similar. Rome never

---

[125] Ibid., 64
[126] Ibid., 93
[127] Regan, 31

again ventured into Germany, and the border between France and Germany was established at the Rhine River. Most significant was that Germany was not a Roman province. Germany was free to determine its own destiny. Later, there would be Anglo-Saxon raids into Britain and, therefore, England became Anglo-Saxon, free of Roman influence. If the German tribes had been pacified in AD 9, would they have later raided Rome in the 4th and 5th centuries?

In AD 9, Rome had the strength to invade Germany and pacify the tribesmen, but this would have required a major effort. Rome, at the time, was spread very thin. Its empire extended from Britain in the north and to North Africa in the south. It also extended from Spain in the west to Turkey in the east. Rome was forced to include barbarians in its ranks to fill-out the Roman Army. To invade Germany would require the call-up of troops from all over the empire. This would weaken their holdings that could cause an uprising in some distant corner of the empire. Thus, the Romans may have reasoned that Germany was not worth the effort. To maintain the empire was a more acceptable goal.

After the battle of Red River, Spain may have reasoned as the Romans. The Comanches were not worth the effort. The Spanish Empire in the New World was larger than the Roman Empire. It extended from the southern tip of South America to the Canadian frontier. A major effort against the Comanches would weaken their holdings in other parts of their vast empire.

The ramifications of the Spanish decision were far reaching. Texas, like Germany in 9 AD, was free to develop without outside interference, and eventually became an independent nation. Texas was later to become part of the United States. Texas entering the Union precipitated the Mexican War. This war resulted in the addition to the United States all the territory between Texas and the Pacific Ocean.

Mostly, Spain had used a mission-presidio system to subdue the hostile wilderness.[128] The Spanish Crown believed that ten years was required to pacify and civilize a tribe. The Spanish term for this method was *reduce.*[129] The function of the mission was to teach Indians the Catholic faith and agricultural pursuits. The presidio or garrison soldiers were to provide protection. The Spanish system worked well in Mexico, New Mexico, and California. In Texas, this system worked only in the area south of San Antonio.

In New Mexico, the Spanish system seemed ideally suited for the Indians living along the upper Rio Grande River. In 1609, a contingent of soldiers and Spanish families under Hidalgo Don Pedro set out from Mexico to establish a capital city in the new Spanish kingdom of New Mexico. When the Spanish arrived, they found about 40,000 Indians that lived in well-planned villages and engaged in agricultural pursuits.[130] The Spaniards called the villages pueblos, and, thus, the Indians became known as Pueblo Indians. These Indians enjoyed the new agricultural crops brought by the Spanish settlers. Mission priests related Biblical tales which the Indians readily

---

[128] Editors, 49
[129] Ibid., 50
[130] Ibid., 50

savored. It seemed that now the Pueblo Indians were *reduced.*

The Spaniards, however, were their own worst enemies. The civil authorities believed they had dominion over the Indians while the priests believed they held ultimate authority. The civil authorities encouraged the Indians to return to their old religions. The priests then punished the Indians for being unfaithful. Once, 47 Indians were charged with witchcraft. Four were hanged in Santa Fe, and the remainder was whipped in public.[131]

One punished Indian, Pope, had always resented the Spanish presence. The Spaniards' unjust rules now gave Pope his opportunity to overthrow the Spanish overlords. He sought out other like-minded Indians. His recruiting drive gained success as a severe drought plagued the area and crops dried up. The neighboring Apache Indians were also affected by the drought. The Apaches solved their food problem by raiding the Pueblo Indians. The Apache raids coupled with the drought and the restrictions imposed by the Spanish overlords produced a swelling Indian discontent. Pope was then ready to strike. In August 1680, Pope launched his surprise attack on the Spaniards. At the time, there were about 2,800 Spaniards living in New Mexico. The Spaniards fought back courageously, but they were overwhelmed by the large number of Indians. After their defeat, the Spaniards were permitted to leave unmolested to the safety of the El Paso mission, which was established in 1659. About 2,000 Spaniards reached the safety of the El Paso mission.[132]

---

[131] Ibid., 51
[132] Ibid., 52

After the victory, the organizer of the Pueblo revolt, Pope, behaved the same as the tyrannical Spaniards. Pope moved into the Spanish governor's palace and declared himself, Governor Pope. He expected the same tributes of goods and services as the Spanish governor. The drought continued, and the Apaches intensified their raids on the pueblos. In 1688, Pope died, and he left a legacy of a poor, weak pueblo community.[133]

Spain, aware of the plight of the Pueblo community, then adopted a plan to reconquer the Pueblo Indians. In 1692, Diego de Vargas, a fearless Spanish leader, assembled a force of 140 men and 60 soldiers in El Paso.[134] He marched north to Santa Fe. Upon arrival, he boldly addressed the Indians who were behind fortifications. He asked the Indians to yield peaceably, and they would be forgiven. After some deliberation, the Indians decided to take a chance and accept Vargas' terms.

New Mexico then became an important province that would become a buffer to protect Mexico from marauding Indians north of the Rio grande.[135] Taos, New Mexico became an important trade center for the Spaniards and Pueblo Indians. The Comanches were invited to the Taos Trade Fairs. The Spaniards and the Comanches believed it was to their advantage to attend these fairs. The Comanches had raided the Pueblo Indians, but found that they could get more goods by trading. The Spanish believed it was better to make peace with the Comanches and eventually enlist their help in warring on their mutual

---

[133] Ibid., 54
[134] Ibid., 54
[135] Ibid., 77

enemy: the Apache Indians. Between 1772 and 1777, 1,674 Spaniards in New Mexico had been killed by marauding Indians.[136]

From 1780 and onward, the Comanches bartered at Taos Trade Fairs.[137] The Comanches brought dried meat, buffalo hides, tallow, salt and horses. The Spanish brought blankets, beads and like items. The Pueblo Indians brought maize, squash, pottery and decorative turquoises.

As the Comanches drove the Apaches into New Mexico, the Apaches then became the Spaniards' most predatory enemy in New Mexico. In 1777, Spanish King Carlos III installed a new governor of New Mexico, Don Juan Bautista de Anza.[138] Anza was explicitly charged to eliminate the Indian menace in New Mexico. Anza became knowledgeable of Indian tribal relationships. He knew that the Comanches were at odds with the Apaches. He became aware also that the Utes and Navajos were enemies of the Apaches. Anza sought to unite the Comanches, Utes and Navajos with the Spaniards to fight the Apaches. Anza was not without resources. He could withhold trade goods that the Indians began to be dependent. He was also authorized by the Crown to bribe the Indians with horses and weapons to obtain good alliances.

One element influencing an alliance with the Comanches was the disposition of the Louisiana territory. Louisiana, an 885,000 square mile area that extended from the mouth of the Mississippi River to the Canadian border, was claimed by France when La Salle floated down the

---

[136] Ibid., 123
[137] Ibid., 55
[138] Ibid., 124

Mississippi River in 1682. France held Louisiana until 1762 when it was then ceded to Spain for being a French ally in the French and Indian War. In 1800, Spain returned Louisiana to France by a secret treaty. In 1803, France sold the Louisiana territory to the United States for $15 million.

In the 17th century, French traders, trappers and missionaries began traveling from the Northeast of North America to the Great Lakes and then down the Mississippi River.[139] They also journeyed over Mississippi's tributaries: Red, Arkansas, Missouri, and Kansas Rivers. Here they could trade with the Plains Indians. The French traders sought animal furs, dried meat, buffalo hides and deerskins from the Indians. In turn, the Indians received textiles, metal tools, knives, awls, needles, hoes, pots, pans, and firearms with ammunition.[140] The last two items made the Indians more powerful and intractable. Thus, the French traders in Louisiana supplied the Comanches with an essential element in their source of power. The Comanches already had a steady source of horses from Mexico. Horses and firearms made the Comanches the scourge of the South Plains.

When Louisiana became Spanish territory, the source of French firearms began to dry-up. The Comanches were then more willing to join an alliance with Spain; so that they might obtain Spanish firearms and ammunition. As the Comanches were divided into about five divisions, they assumed that the Spanish were also divided into several divisions. Southern Comanches stole horses from Spaniards in Mexico and traded them to Western

---

[139] Rollings, 49
[140] Ibid., 51

Comanches who in turn traded them to Spaniards in New Mexico. The Spaniards in New Mexico were aware of the sources of horses that were being traded, but believed it was better to maintain good relations with the Comanches. The Comanches, moreover, were reliable allies in the ongoing struggle with the Apaches. The Spaniards also benefitted from the trade goods brought by the Comanches to the Taos Trade Fairs. Horse thievery in Mexico was simply Mexico's problem.

The Spaniards also realized that if they could not enter the Comancheria, neither could any other expansionist power. They were concerned about French and later English intrusions. Dr. Rupert Richardson, a Comanche historian, concluded, "The Comancheria as a barrier was worth more to Spain than all the troops she had in New Mexico."[141]

New Mexico thrived under this policy. The New Mexico Kingdom was considered the most stable province of the Spanish West. In 1777, it had a Spanish population of about 7,000. At the census of 1799, the Spanish population had increased to 18,826.[142]

New Mexico stood at the center of Spanish claims north of the Rio Grande. It was central to all Spanish territories westward to the Pacific and eastward to the Mississippi. Strategically, Spain believed that New Mexico must be strengthened to protect the more productive states of Coahuila and Sonora in Mexico.[143] As the century grew to

---

[141] Richardson, 23
[142] Editors, 131
[143] Ibid. 124

a close, however, Spain's fortunes in the New World began a fundamental change.

In 1776, the thirteen English colonies in the New World declared their independence from England. Although Spain ruled by royal decree as did England, it did not champion independence movements. However, here was an opportunity to strike at its old adversary. Therefore, it sided with the American revolutionaries as did France. Unlike France, though, Spain did not actively support the Americans. At the Treaty of Versailles, which ended the American Revolutionary War in 1783, Spain did gain its old province of Florida, which it had lost to Britain in the French and Indian War.

Florida would be the last territorial gain that Spain would obtain in the New World. Events in France would undo Spain's hold in the New World. A year after America adopted its constitution, the French people rose up to overthrow their government. The French Revolution took place between 1789 and 1799 and produced Napoleon Bonaparte. Napoleon was to have a profound impact on Spain's New World possessions.

In 1783, the thirteen English colonies in America gained their independence from England and became the United States. Spain soon realized that the ubiquitous Americans were more of a menace to their New World holdings than the English or French. In 1797, one half the population of Louisiana was American who completely disregarded all laws of illegal immigration. Spain then realized that it could not control Louisiana. In 1800, therefore, at the Treaty of Ildefenso, Spain ceded Louisiana to France. The treaty specifically included a proviso that no English speaking government would ever own

Louisiana. Napoleon, however, needed money to finance his European wars.[144] In 1803, he found a willing buyer and sold Louisiana to the United States for $15 million.

Napoleon still had more plans for Spain. At the Bayonne Conference in 1808, Napoleon forced Spain's King Ferdinand to abdicate and then replaced him with Napoleon's brother, Joseph. This act created a tumult in Spain's New World holdings. Spanish upper class émigrés, *gachupines*, held allegiance to Ferdinand. The Creoles, however, resented the authority of the *gachupines* and always believed they were incompetent. Napoleon's action may have just created the spark that ignited Spain's New World holdings into revolution.

Between 1810 and 1826, Spain lost most of its holdings in the New World because of the independence movement. Though, it did sell Florida to the United States for $5 million in 1819.[145] Mexico gained its independence in 1821. The conditions in Texas, though, did not change. Mexico could do nothing more with the Comanches than could Spain. The Comanches were the masters of Texas. It was fait accompli.

Louisiana still hung heavy on the affairs in Texas. In 1803, when Louisiana was acquired by the United States, about 25,000 Americans already occupied the land.[146] After acquisition, thousands more came to inhabit Louisiana. The new settlers needed horses, which the Comanches would readily trade for firearms and ammunition. The Comanches were then no longer

---

[144] Ibid., 95
[145] Nevin, *The Texans*, 16
[146] Editors, 95

dependent upon the Spanish in New Mexico for firearms. The Comanches became more independent and hostile.[147]

The hostility of the Comanches became aggravated as the Americans moved westward from the Atlantic. The westward movement in turn pushed the native Indian population out ahead of them. Between 1825 and 1840, thousands of eastern Indians were relocated near the Comancheria.[148] Also, the Indian Removal Act was signed into law by President Andrew Jackson in 1830. It was at this time that the infamous Trail of Tears occurred.[149] Some 12,000 Cherokee Indians were forced from their homes in the Great Smokey Mountains to the newly established Indian Territory, now known as Oklahoma. Though, some resettled in East Texas. This was a 1,200 mile trek that took the lives of about 4,000 Cherokee Indians. Most died of cholera, measles and exposure.

The new Indian settlers that moved into the Indian Territory took game animals that would have been taken by the Comanches. The food deficiency could only be made up by increased raids into Mexico. The Comanche raids into Mexico began to strike deeper and last longer than before. At first, the raids into Mexico lasted only a few days. Later, the raids lasted weeks and eventually months. The Comanche raids were not limited to the Mexican states along the Rio Grande, such as Coahuila, Chihuahua and Nuevo Leon. In time, they raided Zacatecas, which is about 500 miles south of Comanche Springs, now called Fort Stockton, Texas. On one raid into Mexico, the

---

[147] Richardson, 30
[148] Ibid. 32
[149] Griffin-Pierce, 58 & 59

Comanches were reported to have seen bright plumed birds and tiny men with tails climbing trees.[150] This would indicate that they had raided as far south as the Yucatan Peninsula, an additional 1,000 miles.

When Mexico gained its independence from Spain, Comanche Indian raids were only one of many of its problems. Apache Indians also raided Mexico from bases in New Mexico. The greatest problem facing Mexico was in forming a viable government. Liberals wanted a federation of autonomous states, while the conservatives wanted a strong central government. The Mexican Congress could not settle the issue and the government became fractious. The government was heading toward chaos. Finally, Colonel Agustin de Iturbide, a leader in the fight for independence, dissolved the Congress and declared himself Emperor Agustin I in May 1822.[151]

Another leader in the fight for independence, Antonio Lopez de Santa Anna, was a clever opportunist that switched allegiances whenever it favored his personal designs. In 1822, Santa Ana was a brigadier general. In December of that year, Santa Anna led a force of 400 soldiers, which were personally loyal to him, through the streets of Veracruz. Santa Anna proclaimed Mexico a republic and declared a revolution to overthrow Iturbide's centralist empire. The revolution rapidly gained support. The people wanted a definite change in government. An emperor was the same as being ruled by Spanish

---

[150] Capps, 54
[151] Editors, 98

gachupines. By February 1823, Iturbide was forced to flee into exile.[152]

A liberal Congress was formed, as the liberal federalists were in the majority.[153] After a few months, the Congress drew up a national constitution that had borrowed heavily from the American Constitution. A viable government was formed, and every citizen was to have equal justice and look forward to a better life.

Santa Anna, though, had other plans. He frequently declared, "Man is nothing; power is everything."[154] Santa Anna bided his time and awaited his opportunity. Until then, he supported the liberal cause.

Meaningful events in Mexico paralleled events in Texas at about the same time. Moses Austin, an American from Missouri, saw an opportunity to make money in Texas through a Real Estate venture. He believed his plan would be beneficial to Spain and himself. Spanish people did not have the desire to settle in Texas, as life in Texas was hard and dangerous. In 1820, after three centuries of Spanish colonization, the Spanish population in Texas numbered about 3,500.[155] San Antonio, the major Texas community had a population of about 800 people who lived on the edge of desperation. They lived in crude log huts chinked with mud.[156] Furthermore, Louisiana, on the Texas border, was now American, which would mean American filibusters would readily cross into Texas. With this knowledge,

---

[152] Ibid., 99
[153] Nevin, *The Texans*, 33
[154] Ibid., 64
[155] Ibid., 16
[156] Ibid., 22

Moses believed he could convince the Spanish authorities in Texas to support his plan.

Texas like Louisiana was a mere place name on a map. Neither territory ever really belonged to any nation. Louisiana was a vast unknown territory until President Thomas Jefferson in 1804 appointed two explorers, Lewis and Clark, to follow the Missouri and Columbia Rivers to the Pacific Ocean.

Texas had a similar but less deliberate experience. Spanish conquistadores, searching for gold, stumbled into Texas. Cabeza de Vaca, shipwrecked off the Texas coast, by chance journeyed through southern Texas in 1530.[157] Francisco de Coronado, in 1540, passed through present day Amarillo, Texas searching for the elusive seven cities of gold. In 1600, Juan de Onate followed closely the route traveled by Coronado. The conquistadores were only interested in gold. Since Texas had no gold, they had no interest in Texas.

In October 1820, Austin set out to San Antonio to meet with the Spanish Governor of Texas, Antonio de Martinez. At first, Martinez would not meet with Austin, but Austin's old friend, Baron de Bastrop who by chance was in San Antonio, interceded in Austin's behalf. Bastrop, who maintained a friendship with the governor, showed the governor the Spanish passport obtained by Austin when Missouri was a part of Spanish Louisiana. This saved the day for Austin. Martinez then agreed to meet with him.[158]

Austin could explain that he represented 300 American families that were sympathetic to Spain and wanted to

---

[157] Editors, 36
[158] Nevin, *The Texans*, 22

settle permanently in Texas. They would raise cotton, corn, and sugar. Austin stressed that the new American settlers in Texas would become Spanish citizens,[159] and as land holders they would defend Texas against illegal American filibusters and hostile Indians. They would pledge allegiance to the King of Spain. In May 1821, the commandant general in Texas sent word to Austin that his Texas plan had been approved and was granted 200,000 acres of his choice.[160]

Spain perceived more than Austin of Spain's desperation. Spain was rapidly losing its position as a world power. It no longer had the resources of money or people to hold its vast empire. Texas was needed as a buffer to protect New Mexico and Northern Mexico. If Spain could not find loyal Spaniards to populate Texas, Americans loyal to Spain would have to fulfill the need. Also, American settlers in East Texas would be closer to the Comancheria than Northern Mexico. Might the Comanches more likely then to attack settlements in East Texas than Northern Mexico?

Later in the year, two critical events emerged as if to dash Austin's Texas real estate venture. On June 10, Moses Austin died of pneumonia and on June 30, Mexico became independent from Spain. Before he died, however, Moses Austin had kept his oldest son, Stephen, apprized of his Texas venture. He had hoped Stephen would join him in this venture, but Stephen had remained only lukewarm. Moses Austin would not be outdone. He was aware of his son's character. Before he died, he called his wife to his

---

[159] Ibid., 16
[160] Ibid., 24

bedside and said, "Tell Stephen to take my place, and if God in his wisdom thought best to disappoint him in the accomplishment of his plans formed for the benefit of the family, he prayed him to extend his goodness to you and to enable you to go on with the business in the same way he would have done."[161] Moses judged his son accurately. Stephen would not deny his father's deathbed request and whole heartedly supported his father's Texas venture. On July 15, 1821, he entered Texas and proceeded to San Antonio.

Fortunately for Stephen, the governor of Texas remained the same after Mexican independence. Governor Martinez cordially received Stephen Austin as the heir to his father's grant. Baron de Bastrop was on hand to assist Stephen. Austin's Texas venture went forward smoothly. He explored the area east of San Antonio and decided upon a location 175 miles east of San Antonio and 65 miles north of the Gulf Coast for his colony. His settlement would be named: San Felipe de Austin.

Just as matters were moving forward for Austin, he received disastrous news. In May 1822, the liberal Mexican government was overthrown and replaced by an emperor, Agustin Iturbide. Austin's colonization plan of Texas had to be requested again. This time, Austin had to travel to Mexico City where he found a factious government divided between a centralist government and liberal federalists who wanted more autonomy for the states. At first, the emperor denied Austin's request, but in January 1823, he relented.

---

[161] Ibid., 24

Austin felt that his patience had been rewarded. Again, however, the Mexican government changed. Iturbide was driven into exile, and a liberal government replaced the emperor. Austin had to petition the Mexican government again. Stephen F. Austin is known as the Father of Texas. The title could not have been more appropriate. After a year in Mexico City, Austin's colony was finally approved by the new Congress on April 11, 1823.

The Mexican government stipulated two things for the new settlers: they must become citizens of Mexico and become Roman Catholics. Citizenship was not a problem for the new settlers. They were more interested in land that they could work and upon which they could build their lives and families and had almost no interest in politics. The church was a different matter. Most of the new settlers were Protestant. The Mexican government, though, was not insistent upon church rites. However, the new colonists were not to flaunt their Protestantism by erecting Protestant churches.

Austin returned to San Felipe and his colony began to flourish. By 1830, his colony had about 4,000 settlers. Mexico then permitted other American colonizers or *empresarios* to bring more settlers to eastern Texas.[162] The most noted were Hayden Edwards and Green DeWitt. There were now some 16,000 Americans in Texas.[163] During this time, no additional Mexicans migrated to Texas. Thus, the American population outnumbered the Mexican population by more than four to one. The culture of eastern Texas was decidedly American.

---

[162] Rollings, 60
[163] Nevin, *The Texans*, 36

These colonists settled in East Texas east of the Colorado River, which was well out of Comanche territory and the Comanche trails raiding into Mexico.[164] They did, however, encounter Karankawa Indians. The Karankawas resented the newcomers, as they took game animals that would have been theirs. There were many bloody encounters, and some settlers were killed. The Mexican government could not provide the military or police units for the East Texas colonists. Austin was then obligated by the Mexican government to form local defense units for his colony. Attacks by the Karankawas made eager volunteers of most men in the colony. Tactics by the militia units soon changed from static defense to wide-ranging horse patrols in hot pursuit.[165] They sought out Indian encampments and attacked them. The name of these horse patrols evolved from "ranging companies" to ultimately Texas Rangers. They attacked renegade Indians and outlaws with equal vigor.

A little known story of Stephen Austin and his encounter with Comanches in Mexico is intriguing. While on a trip to Mexico City, Austin was captured by Comanches and relieved of his horses and baggage.[166] When it was discovered that Austin was an American, the Comanches released him unharmed and returned his baggage and horses. He was sent on his way, but the Indians did retain his Spanish grammar book.

The new colonists in East Texas were left to govern themselves. As Americans they expected roads, schools,

---

[164] Rollings, 60
[165] Nevin, *The Texans*, 33
[166] Rollings, 60

post offices and courts to be established by their government. Mexico, at the time, was unstable and could provide little more than advice. The liberal government, which was in control in 1825, passed a law that was somewhat beneficial to Texas. It established the capital of Texas and the north Mexican state of Coahuila to be located in Saltillo, 500 miles from San Felipe. This was much closer than Mexico City, but it did not address the problems associated with Texas. Also, travel in the area at this time was very primitive. A trip from San Felipe to Saltillo required several overnight camps on the trail. Travelers had to be wary of marauding Indians and bandits. On one trip to Mexico City, Stephen Austin disguised himself as a beggar to elude bandits.

Texas was not treated as a separate entity but was part of Coahuila. The combined states were known as Coahuila y Texas. Texas and Cohuila were two separate and distinct wholes. Coahuila had been under Spanish rule since the Spanish conquest of Mexico. It could now readily become part of the new Mexican nation. Texas, on the other hand, was never under Spanish rule but was a vast territory inhabited by wild and aggressive Indians. It was now being populated by a dynamic and vigorous people with an entirely different culture. Stephen Austin was loyal to Mexico and did his duties as *empresario* with diligence. However, he would require support from the Mexican government.

Support, though, was not forthcoming. In 1824, Mexico had adopted a liberal constitution that promulgated a democratic government with some power to the states.[167]

---

[167] Nevin, *The Texans*, 62

The centralists, though, were never eliminated and power vacillated between the Federalists and Centralists. The country was near civil war.

The Mexican Constitution proclaimed justice for all. Unfortunately, the political-social order held over from Spanish rule still held Mexico in its grip. The *gachupines* left with Spanish rule. Instead of four tiers in the social-political order, there were now three tiers: Spaniards born in Spain and Mexico in the first tier, mestizos in the second tier and pure-blood Indians in the bottom tier. Freedom and equality were applied only to people within a class and never crossed class lines.

In 1828, Centralist, Anastacio Bustamante, headed the Mexican government. Bustamante became alarmed when he learned that the American population of Texas east of San Antonio and Goliad now outnumbered Mexicans by ten to one.[168] On April 6, 1830, the centralist government decreed a military occupation of Texas and an end to all American immigration.

In 1831, mercenary Colonel John Davis Bradburn, an American in Mexican service, entered Anahuac, Texas and for no apparent reason ordered the American settlement of Liberty to be abolished.[169] The settlers were angered by this act and protested vociferously. The more outspoken settlers were put under arrest. As Americans, they could not accept such injustice. A short skirmish ensued and ten settlers and five soldiers were killed.

The American settlers feared Mexican retribution. However, they learned that Santa Anna, a Federalist, was

---

[168] Ibid., 62
[169] Ibid., 65

conducting a military campaign to unseat Bustamante. Subsequently, they learned that Santa Anna was successful. The settlers now believed they had found a champion who would be sympathetic to their needs and desires. The settlers wanted an end to the anti-immigration act of 1830 and separate statehood for Texas.[170]

On April 1, 1833, the settlers met in convention in San Felipe. Besides statehood and anti-immigration, the settlers added a constitution and a bicameral legislature. The convention chose Austin to deliver a draft of the constitution to Santa Anna in Mexico City.

Unrelated to political events in Texas but nonetheless quite significant was the arrival, at this time, of a special emissary from President Andrew Jackson of the United States: Sam Houston. Sam Houston was a close friend and confident of Andrew Jackson. He crossed the Red River into Texas from Indian Territory, now Oklahoma, on December 2, 1832. Houston carried a special passport that directed him to confer with certain Comanche chiefs that would be found near San Antonio. Houston was directed to seek a peace treaty between the Comanches and Indian tribes in Indian Territory.[171] Along the way to San Antonio, Houston stopped in Nacogdoches and San Felipe where he met his old friend, Jim Bowie, and a new friend, Stephen Austin.

Houston did meet with some Comanche chiefs but the talks were inconclusive. Houston then opened a law practice in Nacogdoches, at the time, the largest town in Texas. This was somewhat surprising as Nacogdoches was

---

[170] Ibid., 65
[171] Ibid., 51

abandoned a decade earlier.[172]   Nacogdoches became the jumping off place for most new American settlers coming to Texas. Houston had practiced law in the United States. He now studied Mexican law and could give legal advice to Americans wanting land in Texas.[173]

Austin arrived in Mexico City in July 1833, to present the proposals of the San Felipe Convention.[174] He found the city in turmoil and could not find any government official to meet with him.   After almost three months without a meeting, Austin, out of disgust, lost his patience with the government in Mexico City. He fired off an imprudent letter to the city council in San Antonio. Austin declared, "The fate of Texas depends upon itself and not upon this government. The country is lost if its inhabitants do not take its affairs into their own hands."[175] Austin had misjudged the loyalty of the San Antonio city council, which concluded that Austin wanted Texas independence. Austin's letter was forwarded to Mexico City.

Because of the general turmoil in Mexico, Austin's letter was slow in its travel from San Antonio to Mexico City. Austin met with Santa Anna who granted a repeal of the anti-immigration law but nothing else. Shortly after Austin left Mexico City for Texas, his imprudent letter arrived. He was ordered arrested and thrown into a Mexico City jail. While in Mexico City, Austin could observe the Mexican government and its leader, Santa Anna, first hand.[176]

---

[172] Ibid., 16
[173] Ibid., 68
[174] Ibid., 68
[175] Ibid., 68
[176] Ibid., 69

After about two years, Austin was released from prison. He returned to San Felipe an entirely changed man. Austin, always loyal to Mexico, had been conciliatory to Mexico. He often explained the difference between American and Mexican laws and reiterated overall Mexican goodwill. Austin had pledged to fulfill obligations as a Mexican citizen and his duty as an *empresario*.[177]

Now, Austin declared, "Santa Anna is a base, unprincipled bloody monster... War is our only recourse. No halfway measures, but war in full."[178] It may have seemed that Austin had overreacted. Santa Anna, though, frequently announced, "Were I made God, I should wish to be something more."[179] Santa Anna had been elected to head a liberal government. However, after ten months in office, and much duplicity and betrayal of associates, Santa Anna dismissed the liberal Congress and replaced it with one subservient to him. His vice president was forced into exile. He then moved to completely crush federalism.[180]

War came to Texas. Texas and eight other Mexican states reacted to support the Liberal Constitution of 1824. They did not want complete independence but wanted to be part of Mexico under the Constitution of 1824. Santa Anna would not have any of this. He ordered his troops to sack the capital of Zacatecas, an avowed federalist state. Coahuila, another federalist state, was next. The government in Saltillo fled toward Texas but was intercepted by Mexican troops.

---

[177] Ibid., 66
[178] Ibid., 71
[179] Ibid., 64
[180] Editors, 99

Texas was next. Santa Anna, himself, would lead the punitive expedition into Texas. Texas had many willing men who would fight but few had any military experience. An army, if it expects to win, must have discipline and the ability to fight as a unit. Without discipline, a group of fighting men becomes a mob, which can readily be defeated by disciplined troops. The Texans, fortunately, had a military man and recognized leader who came to them at the most critical moment: Sam Houston.

Texas was indeed fortunate to have an excellent military leader on hand at its most crucial moment. Stephen Austin with his tact and diplomatic skills came forward after his father died. Now, Houston with his leadership and military skills came forward at a time when Texas sorely needed military leadership. Without these two men, Texas would probably still be Coahuila y Texas.

The Texans, at first, won several minor skirmishes, but then suffered badly after Santa Anna was at the head of his army. The Texans lost every man at the Battle of the Alamo in San Antonio and later every man at Goliad. After the Battle of the Alamo, Santa Ana divided his army into three columns and marched eastward.[181] If any column found the remnants of the Texas Army, it was to signal the other two columns to move together in a coordinated attack.

The Texas Army, under Sam Houston, numbered about 800 men. The army retreated eastward to a plain near Houston. Here they planned the unexpected: attack. Santa Anna held overwhelming numerical superiority, and, therefore, his army was to attack and the Texans defend.

---

[181] Nevin: *The Texans*, 119

The Texans were now able to attack the center Mexican column, commanded by Santa Anna himself. Since the Mexican Army was divided into three columns, the Texans would face only twelve hundred Mexican soldiers in the center column.[182]

The battle, on the plain of San Jacinto, lasted only eighteen minutes. It was an overwhelming victory for Texas. The attack by the Texans was a complete surprise, as the other two Mexican columns were not alerted in time to join in the battle. Santa Anna was held hostage and was ordered to march all Mexican forces out of Texas. In exchange for his life, he was ordered to recognize the independence of Texas. The duplicitous Santa Anna would willingly sign anything.[183]

After Santa Anna was released from his Texas guards, he returned to Mexico. He never really recognized Texas independence and small skirmishes between Texas and Mexico continued for the next ten years.[184] Texas, however, was recognized as a republic by the United States on March 3, 1837. Thereafter, recognition was soon followed by France, Britain, Netherlands and Belgium.[185]

Texas was then well on its way to becoming a viable nation. New immigrants from the United States poured into Texas by the thousands. Texas offered free land to each new settler, and the population of Texas grew from about 35,000 in 1836 to over 140,000 in 1847. Immigrants from Europe also settled in Texas at this time.[186]

---

[182] Ibid. 128
[183] Ibid.: 141
[184] Ibid.: 141
[185] Ibid., 210 & 214
[186] Ibid., 156

As the new immigrants moved into eastern Texas, they displaced the Indians living there. These Indians were forced westward to the edge of the Comancheria. Some Cherokees, forced from their homes in the Eastern United States, also had migrated to Texas. The Comanches then had to deal with more hostile Indians on their eastern frontier. A source of food became a paramount concern. The newly displaced Indians took game animals that should have been for the Comanches.

Consequently, the Comanches and the displaced Indians became more hostile toward each other and the new American settlers. As the food supply within the Comancheria dwindled, the Comanches increased their raids into Mexico. Besides food, the Comanches had an additional incentive to raid Mexico: trade goods. The new settlers in Texas needed horses, and other items that were readily found in the North Mexican states of Coahuila, Chihuahua, and Nuevo Leon.[187]

Mexico, south of the Comancheria, was ideally suited for Comanche raids. The area west of the Comancheria was the mountains of New Mexico. Mountain warfare was quite different from fighting on the plains. In mountain warfare, stealth and concealment on foot was the utmost essentials required. On the open plains, the Comanches could use their superior horsemanship skills to strike swiftly and in mass.

In the east were the cross timbers and the woods of eastern Texas. Fighting in wooded areas was much like fighting in mountains. Stealth and concealment were the prescribed tactics.

---

[187] Richardson, 97

In the north were aggressive Indians much like the Comanches that would not easily be defeated. More telling was that Indians north of the Comancheria were not endowed with an abundant supply of horses. Northern raids would, therefore, not prove as productive as raids into Mexico.

Mexico, south of the Comancheria, was much like the West Texas home of the Comanches. It was a dry central plateau from five thousand to eight thousand feet in elevation. It lay between two mountain ranges: Sierra Madre Occidental and Sierra Madre Oriental. An organized raid into Mexico might originate at Comanche Springs and then move south through the Persimmon Gap of the Chios Mountains of Texas. After leaving the Chios Mountains, the Comanches would then be in Northern Mexico. Another route was to follow the Rio Grande River south of San Antonio and then cross the river into Mexico.

In time, the aggressive Comanches would clash with the equally aggressive Texans. While the Texans remained in East Texas, there was no trouble between the Comanches and the Texans. The Texas government realized, however, that if Texas was to survive, it must expand its domain beyond East Texas. To strengthen the new republic, Texas had to increase its population with more independent self-reliant people.

The new nation was also badly in need of money. All it had was land. It could follow the example set by the United States and sell land at $1.25 per acre. To compete with the United States, Texas would first have to entice new settlers to emigrate to Texas by giving away free land. At first, each new family in Texas received two square miles of land. Later, free land was reduced to 320 acres,[188] which was still a considerable amount. This land policy caused the Texas population to rabidly increase. The new growth caused the western frontier to move westward into the Comancheria.

The land in Texas was not only plentiful but also productive, which beckoned even more people to Texas. An East Texas farm could produce 80 bushels of corn or 2,000 pounds of cotton per acre.[189] A newcomer to Texas exalted, "Texas is full of enterprising and persevering people. The timid and lazy generally return to the States."[190] The Texans became a special breed of people after independence: proud, independent, self-reliant, optimistic, and confident.

Sam Houston was elected president of the Texas Republic, which was modeled after the United States. Houston was aware of Texas' financial limitations and followed a conservative course. He disbanded the army, as the republic had no funds to pay its soldiers. However, the Texas Congress instituted a militia.

Every able-bodied male between the ages of 17 and 50 was required to serve in the militia.[191] One day each month every male in the militia was required to train with his company. Men in the militia knew their responsibility and that their friends and family depended on them to do their duty. The militia was augmented by some hard core professionals: Texas Rangers. The Rangers were formed in

---

[188] Nevin, *The Texans*, 156
[189] Ibid., 148
[190] Ibid., 155
[191] Ibid., 174

1835 to specifically fight the Comanches.[192]   They were paid $1.25 per day. The Rangers and the disciplined militia were credited with being the principal organizations that held Texas together.

Texas, at the time, required self-disciplined law enforcement men with integrity. A Texas Ranger alone or in twos and threes would readily take any assignment. Many law breakers in the United States sought sanctuary in Texas, but they were quickly ferreted-out by the Texas Rangers. Texas would be permitted to grow without fear of lawless marauders.

Heretofore, the Comanches encountered only a few Texans. With the increasing population of Texas, though, new immigrants crossed into the Comancheria.   The Comanches then believed it would be to their best interest to come to some accommodation with the Texans.   In February 1838, 150 Comanche warriors rode into San Antonio and requested that a party of citizens go with them to their camp and make a treaty of peace. A group of San Antonio citizens, including Texas Congressman Mosely Baker, accepted the Indian's offer and rode with them to their camp. Here the Texans were kindly received, and they met with 15 Comanche leaders.   The Comanches' main concern was a definite boundary. The Comanches insisted upon "full and undisputed possession of the country north of the Guadalupe mountains."[193] The Texans would not discuss the boundary question but agreed to talk it over with their government. It was agreed that all parties would meet again in San Antonio for a general council.

---

[192] Ibid., 174
[193] Richardson, 42

The second meeting, May 1838, in San Antonio produced nothing new, but both parties left the meeting in good spirits.

In December 1838, Texas underwent a major change in policy. Texas held a new election for president and Sam Houston could not succeed himself. Houston's vice president, Mirabeau Bonaparte Lamar, was elected president for a three-year term.[194] Lamar had some rather grandiose plans for Texas. For one, he envisioned a Texas Republic that extended to the Pacific Ocean. Also, he insisted upon the recognition of Texas by Mexico, and, if necessary, by force. Above all, he willed a harsh action to all Indians on Texas soil. The Indians were considered *tenants at will* and held no property rights.[195] There was to be no "Indian Country" in Texas.

One of Lamar's first acts was to drive the Cherokees out of East Texas, since they held no legal title to the land they occupied. Sam Houston was particularly incensed by this order. He held a familial relationship with the Cherokees. When he was 17, he ran away from home and lived with the Cherokees for three years. The Cherokee Chief, John Jolly, adopted Houston as his son.[196] In 1817, Houston was appointed the subagent by the U.S. Army for the Cherokees.

In July 1839, Texas forces engaged the Cherokees in several bloody encounters. Eventually, the Cherokees were driven into the United States' Indian Territory. On the

---

[194] Nevin, *The Texans*, 210
[195] Ibid. 210
[196] Ibid., 52

second day of fighting, Cherokee Chief Bowl was killed. He still held the sword given to him by Sam Houston.

During this time, the Comanches, for the most part, had few encounters with the Texans. The Comanches, though, still wanted an accommodation with the Texans. They hoped Texas would recognize a boundary between the Comanches and the Texans. On January 10, 1840, three Comanches rode into San Antonio and presented themselves to Colonel Henry W. Karnes of the Texas Rangers. Karnes advised that there could be no peace until the Comanches released all of their white captives. The Indians agreed with this request and would return later for a general council.

Karnes, motivated by the Lamar tenet of driving Indians out of Texas, had other plans. He suggested that the Indian delegation be met with "a force sufficient to justify our seizing and retaining those who may come in, as hostages for the delivery of such American captives as may at this time be among them."[197]

On March 19, 1840, the Comanche's delegation, 65 men, women and children, returned to San Antonio. They brought only one prisoner, Matilda Lockhart.[198] The Texans demanded more prisoners, as they believed that the Indians held about 200 people captured in Texas settlements.[199] The Indians explained that other Comanche bands held the other prisoners, and these must be negotiated separately. This was not acceptable to the

---

[197] Richardson, 49
[198] Ibid., 50
[199] Capps., 30

Texans who then set about to imprison the Indians. In the ensuing struggle seven Texans and 35 Indians were killed.

Such treachery could not go unpunished. The Comanches then planned a major strike in Texas. To do this, they first had to make peace with the Cheyenne, an enemy on the northern frontier of the Comancheria. The Comanches wisely sought a war on only one front. To achieve the desired peace, the Comanches instructed their Kiowa allies, who were noted for being friendly and peaceable, to send peace feelers to the Cheyenne. The Cheyenne, for their part, desired horses, which the Comanches held in abundance. Peace would be to their advantage.

The Cheyenne agreed to meet the Comanches to make peace. The meeting was held near the Flint Arrowpoint River in present day Kansas. The meeting and the following general council took several days to complete. Indian protocol demanded the showing of goodwill. Rational dialog was inadequate in the Indian culture. Gifts that were not only valuable but also needed would wipe away old grievances and pave the way for lasting peace. The Comanches brought enough horses for every Cheyenne that could ride.[200] Some Cheyenne got six or more. The Cheyenne reciprocated with kettles, beads, blankets, calico and firearms. After the peace council on the Arrowpoint, the tribes never made war on each other again.

Once peace was established on its northern periphery, the Comanches had only to face one enemy: a warlike group of white men called Texans.[201] Early in August

---

[200] Ibid., 35
[201] Ibid., 30

1840, the Comanches launched a major strike into East Texas. Some 500 warriors from several Comanche bands bypassed San Antonio and struck southeast where they attacked the town of Victoria and then Linville on the Gulf Coast. Twenty-four Texans were killed and more would have been killed if the people of Linville had not taken flight in boats.[202] The Comanches came away with two thousand horses and other booty and then headed for their sanctuary in West Texas.

News of the raid quickly spread to nearby parts of East Texas. The Texas Rangers and the militia in Austin, Bastrop and Gonzales quickly organized to cut off the retreating Comanches. The Texans found the Comanches at the forks of Plumb Creek, which is near the town of Lockhart. They immediately attacked the Comanches and put them to rout. In the ensuing running battle, the Comanches lost most of their booty and left behind 50 dead warriors.[203]

The Texans were not satisfied with the results of the Plumb Creek battle. They believed the Comanches needed further punishment. Whereupon Colonel John H Moore requested volunteers for a punitive expedition against the Comanches. In early October 1840, 90 Texans and 12 Lipan Apache Indians volunteered to serve in Moore's expedition.[204] After about a 300-mile trek, the Lipans sighted a Comanche village of about 60 families and 125 warriors. The Texans waited for night and then launched a furious attack that was a complete surprise to the

---

[202] Richardson, 52
[203] Ibid., 52
[204] Ibid., 52

Comanches. The Comanches lost 130 dead and 34 captives. The Texans came away with 500 horses. The attack had good results, as the Comanches reduced the number of attacks on Texas settlements.

For the remainder of 1840 and into 1841, Texas' problems with Indians were nominal. President Lamar, though, still envisioned grand schemes for Texas. He wanted Texas to participate in the lucrative trade established on the Santa Fe Trail between Missouri and New Mexico. He also believed that New Mexico, a part of Mexico, would prefer to be part of Texas. Thus, a caravan of 300 men and 21 wagons left Austin for Santa Fe in June 1841. The governor of New Mexico, however, was an appointee of Santa Anna, and the Texans were met with a strong military force that disarmed the Texans and imprisoned them.[205] The Texans had traveled through the Comancheria where they were attacked by Comanches. When they arrived in New Mexico, they were not ready for another battle in their weakened condition.

Fortunately for Texas, Lamar's term as president expired at the end of 1841, and Sam Houston was again elected as president for a three-year term. Houston then addressed Congress: "There is not a dollar in the treasury. We are not only without money, but without credit, and for want of punctuality without honor." Houston counseled the citizens of Texas, "The truest interest of Texas is to maintain peace with all nations and cultivate the soil."[206] Thereupon, Houston cut his own salary in half, abolished positions and consolidated departments. He refused to pay

---

[205] Nevin, *The Texans*, 215
[206] Ibid., 216

for an army. The militia would be expected to continue to do its duty. In the previous three-year administration, the government spent $5,000,000. During Houston's administration the government would spend $500,000.

Houston would have some difficulty in maintaining expenses. In March 1842, Santa Anna sent a Mexican force across the Rio Grande and occupied San Antonio, Goliad and Victoria. The Mexicans raised the Mexican flag and departed after few days. This act inflamed the Texas Congress, but Houston vetoed a declaration of war.[207]

After a few months, war talk subsided in Congress. Then in September 1842, Santa Anna sent another force of 1,400 men that captured San Antonio. This time, Texas retaliated. A 600-man force of Texas Rangers and militia waited for an opportunity and then ambushed the Mexicans near Salado Creek.[208] The Mexican lost 60 men and the Texans one. The Texans then followed the defeated Mexican unit back to the Rio Grande.

While Houston tried to minimize problems with Mexico, he also sought peace with the Indians, principally the Comanches. Early in 1842, he sent scouts to inform the Indians that the new chief of Texas was a friend of all Indians and wanted lasting peace. The scouts had first to overcome the treachery administered at the council in San Antonio in 1840.

Houston ordered Colonel J.C. Eldredge, Superintendent of Indian Affairs, to locate the chief of the Penateka Comanches or Southern Comanches. Some Delaware

---

[207] Ibid., 216
[208] Ibid., 216

Indians were included as scouts for the search party. A year later, Eldredge found Pah-hah-yo-ko, a leader of the Penateka Comanches. Eldredge explained that Lamar was a "bad chief" and Houston, the present chief who ruled in Texas, was a good chief and friend of the Indian. He presented two Indian prisoners and gifts to show good faith. He also presented the Comanche leader with Houston's letter, which was affixed the Great Seal of the Republic. He then invited the Indians to come to a great council on the Trinity River. On the following day, the chief gave his reply:[209]

> My brother, I have heard your talk and listened to the words your great chief Houston sent me. They are good. I have long desired peace. The children of my people which your chief sent me has made our hearts glad. We know your chief speaks the truth and I am willing to assist him to make the great white path between our different people.

In the Spring of 1844, a council meeting was held on Tehuacana Creek with the lesser Indian tribes of Texas plus representatives from the Southern Comanche band. On the second day of the council, Buffalo Hump, a Comanche leader spoke:

> The Great Spirit above is looking down and sees and hears my talk; the ground is my mother, and sees and hears that I tell the truth. When I first heard the words of your chief, I felt glad; and I was

---

[209] Richardson, 56

uneasy until I struck the white path and came here to see him. That is all I want to say. What I came here for was to hear the words of peace. I have heard them and all is right; peace is peace; I have no more to say.

In general, the council ended with a mutual pledge of peace and friendship. However, the treaty did not include a boundary agreement, which the Comanches believed essential. Also, only the Southern Comanches attended the council. Buffalo Hump explained that the northern Comanche bands were more powerful than his Penateka Comanche band, and he could not be responsible for their actions.[210]

Thereafter, a relative peace was established on the frontier. Peace, though, did not exclude Comanche and Texan trepidations by individuals or small groups. The Comanches and the Texans both felt they had rights to the land. The Comanches believed the Comancheria was their hunting preserve from which they gained food and shelter and to husband their horses. The Texans believed the land should be productive from which homes and families would be built.

Two different cultures vied for supremacy. Each judged the other by their own standards of right and wrong. The Texans believed they were bringing civilization to the frontier. The Comanches were willing to let the Texans live as they wanted in their own land but allow the Comanches to live as they wanted in their land. Both

---

[210] Ibid., 60

cultures seemed to have reasonable expectations but were on a collision course.

Austin was made the capital of Texas in 1839. Comanches, though, continued to prowl its streets. Austin stood on the edge of the Comancheria and an alone late bound citizen often lost his scalp. A citizen of Austin observed, "You were pretty sure to find a congressman at his boarding house after sundown."[211]

In August 1833, a surveyor, Josiah Wilbarger, was scalped by Comanches after being shot through both legs with arrows. Wilbarger survived and lived another twelve years with a partially exposed scull. Wilbarger's brother, John Wesley Wilbarger, then wrote a book, *Indian Depredations in Texas.*[212] He intended to "preserve in history the story of massacres and conflicts with Indians." This book helped shape the attitude of Texans toward Indians. The Texans concluded that Comanches savaged and killed not only men but also women and children.

Savagery cannot be laid on Indians alone. During this period in Texas history, Texas' Shelby county, on the Louisiana border, was particularly noted for violence. Dueling, at the time, was an accepted method of settling grievances. Two men elected to settle their differences with Bowie knives. According to an eyewitness account, "Both men swung forward and both struck a chopping lick as their hands met."[213] One man struck the other's right hand a little above the knuckles, cleaned all the flesh off four fingers clear to the bone, and lodged against his

---

[211] Nevin, *The Texans,* 186
[212] Ibid., 164
[213] Ibid., 174

knuckles. His knife fell to the ground and he was then at the mercy of the other antagonist who only hacked at the defeated man's arms, cleaving the flesh to the elbow on both arms. The loser turned and ran. Nevertheless, the victor followed and cut his shoulder blade in two. He then let him go, declaring that the man was in good condition to behave himself and repent of his evil ways. The eyewitness thought that was a generous act on the victor's part. The victor said he could have killed him, but only wanted to cripple him to make a pious man out of a rogue, a sponger, a horse thief and a peace disturber.

Texas at this time began furiously striving for annexation to the United States. President Houston and most Texans wanted to be annexed to the United States. Most Texans were former Americans and annexation seemed the only natural course. However, there were problems that were not easily resolved. Many Texans owned slaves, which meant that annexation would add another slave state to the United States. The abolitionists' movement was strong enough to override any talk of annexation. Houston then exploited a veiled threat. He made it known that Britain was interested in an independent Texas for trade and sought to employ Texas as a buffer to American expansionism. The United States then became alarmed that Britain and Texas were about to conclude a political alliance. Consequently, the United States quickly approved a resolution to annex Texas on March 1, 1845.[214] President Polk later signed the Texas Admission Act on December 29, 1845.

---

[214] Ibid., 214, 218 & 219

The annexation of Texas by the United States enraged the Mexican government. Mexico's minister in Washington declared, "This legislation is an act of aggression, the most unjust which can be found in the annals of modern history." Mexican newspapers concluded, "The United States desired from the beginning to extend their dominion in such a manner as to become the absolute owners of almost all of this continent. The North American Republic has already absorbed territories pertaining to Great Britain, France, Spain and Mexico. It has employed every means to accomplish this—purchase as well as usurpation, skill as well as force, and nothing has restrained it when treating of territorial acquisition. Louisiana, the Floridas, Oregon and Texas have fallen successively into its power."[215] No acknowledgment was ever conceded that Texas settlers' original desire was for a return to constitutional guarantees made by Mexico in 1824.[216]

On March 8, 1846, an American Army in Corpus Christi, Texas marched south across the Nueces River toward the Rio Grande.[217] Mexico had contended the border between Mexico and Texas was the Nueces River. War was, in the Mexican view, forced upon Mexico. The war lasted seventeen months at a cost of 25,000 Mexican lives and 5,000 Americans.[218] On February 2, 1848, Mexico and the United States signed the peace Treaty of Guadalupe Hidalgo. The main parts of the treaty established the Rio Grande as the border between Texas

---

[215] Editors, 200
[216] Johnson, 56
[217] Editors, 203
[218] Ibid., 224

and Mexico. The United States also added to its territory the present day states of California, Arizona, Nevada, Utah, New Mexico, and part of Colorado. The United States paid Mexico $15 million.[219] An additional proviso of the treaty stipulated that the United States was to restrain Indians from raiding south of the Rio Grande.[220]

The Comanches contended that they never signed the treaty and, therefore, did not agree to stay out of Mexico.[221] According to data, compiled by the Mexican government from 1847 to 1857 in the state of Nuevo Leon, 652 persons were wounded, killed or captured by the Comanches.[222] Other Mexican states: San Luis, Zacatecas, Durango, Chihuahua, Tamaulipas, and Coahuila also suffered but not to the extent of Nuevo Leon. The Comanches were not the only Indian predators from north of the Rio Grande. The Apaches in New Mexico also made raids deep into Mexico.

A traveler who journeyed from Mexico City to Santa Fe in 1846 described the results of a Comanche raid: "For days together I traversed a country completely deserted on this account, passing through ruined villages untrodden for years by the foot of man."[223]

Another account of Comanche raids in northern Mexico was related by an English traveler, George F. Ruxton, in September 1846: "They are now overrunning the whole department of Durango and Chihuahua, have cut off all communications, and defeated, in two pitched battles, the regular troops sent against them. Upward of 10,000 heads

---

[219] Nevin, *The Texans*, 221
[220] Richardson, 100
[221] Ibid., 100
[222] Ibid., 100
[223] Capps, 54

of horses and mules have already been carried off, and scarcely has a hacienda or ranch on the frontier been unvisited, and the people have been killed or captured. The roads are impassable, all traffic is stopped, the ranchos barricaded, and the inhabitants afraid to venture out of their doors. The post and expresses travel at night, avoiding the roads, and intelligence is brought daily of massacres and harryings."[224]

The events in Mexico were similar to a story reaching Europe from a papal envoy, Friar John of Plano Carpini, who passed through Kiev, Russia on his way east six years after the Mongols destroyed the town in 1240, "...We found lying in the field countless heads and bones of dead people; for this city...has been reduced to nothing; barely two hundred houses stand...and...people are held in the harshest slavery."[225]

When planning a raid into Mexico, the Comanches followed two well-known Texas trails. One trail originated in the Texas Panhandle and the other in Western Oklahoma. Both trails crossed at Big Spring, Texas. At the time, there was only a big spring at the location. The big spring as Captain Randolph B. Marcy noted when he traveled through Texas in 1849, "...flowing from a deep chasm in the limestone rocks into an immense reservoir of some fifty feet in depth."[226]

After leaving the big spring, one trail proceeded to Horsehead Crossing over the Pecos River. From here the trail proceeded to Comanche Springs, which was Texas'

---

[224] Richardson, 101
[225] McDowell, 54
[226] Cox, 45

third largest spring. According to an observer in the 1850s, water gushed from the earth "like a sea monster."[227] It is now dry. From Comanche Springs, the trail proceeded to the Persimmon Gap in the Big Bend country and then across the Rio Grande into northern Mexico. The other trail proceeded southeast from the big spring to Las Moras Springs near Brackettville, Texas and then across the Rio Grande into Northern Mexico.

One raid into Mexico, as told by an eyewitness, was led by Buffalo Hump, a Penateka or Southern Comanche, in August 1847. Buffalo Hump with 600 to 800 warriors crossed the Rio Grande near the mouth of the Pecos River.[228] He rode into Coahuila and attacked the areas around Parras and San Fernando. He returned with many horses, mules and a few captives.

As competition for game animals increased, the Comanches raided Mexico more frequently and systematically. Every year in September when the moon was full, the Mexican population could expect an attack from the Comanches. The Mexicans called it the Comanche Moon, and the Comanches called it the Mexican Moon. This was also the time of the "fifth season" in the far southwest part of Texas near the Rio Grande.[229] From mid-August to mid-September, rains come to this desert region which produces an almost overnight growth of plant-life and full water holes. The Comanches needed the water and the plant-life for their horses. Each warrior probably had at least five horses in his remuda. Thus, a

---

[227] Ibid, 50
[228] Richardson, 99
[229] Cox, 42

raiding party of 600 warriors would have as many as 3,000 horses. Horses do not eat meat and, therefore, require a large quantity of grass to make up their comestible requirements.

After a short bivouac, the Comanches then proceeded south across the Rio Grande into northern Mexico. As food became more difficult to find on the Comancheria, the Comanches were forced to raid Mexico more often and for longer periods. Anthropology Professor W.W. Newcomb Jr. said, "Mexico was an easy target and pretty profitable. You've got to support your wives and kids."[230]

The Comanches would then stay in Mexico for four to eight months. They killed all Mexican men they encountered and carried away women and children to barter or enslave. Their big prizes were the thousands of horses and mules found on the ranchos and haciendas. The Comanches then returned to the Comencheria in time for the buffalo hunt.[231]

To honor its treaty obligations of Guadalupe Hidalgo, the United States began building forts on the Comanche trails leading into Mexico. The forts causing the most problems for the Comanches were Fort Clark and Fort Stockton. These forts were placed astride the main watering holes north of the Rio Grande. Fort Clark was established on June 20, 1852[232] and was located near the head of Las Moras Spring. Fort Stockton, which was established on March 23, 1859, was located at Comanche Springs.

---

[230] Ibid., 42

[231] Ibid., 47

[232] Frazer, 146 & 162

These forts forced the Comanches to seek other trails into Mexico. The new trails, though, did not have the water and grass that the old, familiar trails had. Compounding the Comanches' problem was the Texans. The Texans were some warlike people who were as aggressive as themselves. In retaliation, the Comanches then increased their raids on Texans.

The Texans and the military forts were not the only problems confronting the Comanches. After the Mexican War, the Comanches were forced to face, in all, five enemies almost simultaneously. Their new enemies were not now always opposing soldiers, which the Comanches believed they could overcome. Life on the Comancheria became more complex and the Comanches' lifelong guidelines no longer were applicable.

The U.S. Army built forts to protect emigrant wagon trains going west and to protect new settlers in Texas. As the settlers moved into areas near the forts, other settlers moved even farther west. The Army would then build more forts to protect the newer settlers.

The ever encroaching settlers drove lesser Indian tribes from their lands in Texas onto or near the Comancheria.[233] These tribes, mostly Tonkawa, Waco, Wichita, Kickapoo, Delaware, Shawnee, and Cherokee, then competed for food that should be for the Comanches. This in turn forced the Comanches to attack farms and ranches on the Texas frontier to compensate for the loss of game animals in Texas and the enforced curtailed raids into Mexico. By 1866, Comanches and their Kiowa allies raids on Texas ranches were so widespread that only a fifth of the ranches

---

[233] Rollings, 76

on the frontier were being worked.[234] The others were abandoned.

These Indian attacks naturally enraged the Texans. The Texas Rangers and Texas Militia then sought out Indian villages and attacked them. In an encounter in May 1858, the Texans faced 300 Comanche warriors and killed 76 while losing only two killed and three wounded.[235]

The U.S. Army also went over to the offense. General David E. Twiggs, commander of the Western Division of the Army, communicated the following message to the assistant adjutant-general in 1858:

> I would respectfully recommend a change of policy with the Indians. For the last ten years we have been on the defensive. I would suggest that it would be better not to detach the regiment to the posts as formerly, but send two detachments into the Indians' country, and follow them up winter and summer, thus giving the Indians something to do at home in taking care of their families, and they might possibly let Texas alone. I think the experiment worth making…[236]

In 1864, the Army sent a seasoned Indian fighter, Kit Carson, into the Comancheria. His force located two large camps of Kiowas and Comanches on the Canadian River near the site of an old trading post, known as Adobe Walls.

---

[234] "Military History of Texas Map"
[235] Richardson, 119
[236] Ibid., 119

Carson could do little harm, as his force was decidedly outnumbered.[237] He then retreated from the Comancheria.

About this time the United States adopted a policy termed: *pacify*.[238] The Spaniards, who preceded the Americans, used the term, *reduce*, which was another way to force the Indians to conform to a foreign culture. The American policy was brutal and direct. It was designed to force the Indians to live on reservations. The Army was directed to destroy the Indians' winter food supply and capture or kill their horses.[239] General Phil Sheridan, who commanded the Division of the Missouri that contained all the Plains territory between the Canadian border and the Rio Grande, ordered, "Kill or hang all warriors and bring back all women and children."[240]

Another calamitous development occurred that was most devastating to the Plains Indians: the loss of buffalo. In earlier times, the Plains Indians traded a few buffalo hides to European and American traders. In return, the Indians received firearms, tobacco, whiskey and like goods. The traders shipped the hides east where they were made into lap robes. By the 1840s, though, the demand for buffalo hides increased, and the traders were shipping 100,000 buffalo hides a year to the east.[241]

The demand for buffalo hides increased even more when an eastern inventor created a way to convert buffalo hides into conveyor belts for factories.[242] Buffalo hides

---

[237] Rollings, 79
[238] Capps, 194
[239] Ibid., 194
[240] Nevin, *The Soldiers*, 162
[241] Capps, 167
[242] Rollings, 85

were being sold for $3.00 for an ordinary hide and up to $8.00 for choice hides. White hunters with high-powered rifles then began bunting buffalo with tragic efficiency. Only the hides were taken. The meat was usually left to rot on the ground. Sioux Chief White Cloud declared, "Wherever the whites are established, the buffalo is gone, and the red hunters must die of hunger."[243] In 1853, Alfred D. Vaughn, the Indian agent for the upper Missouri stated that about 400,000 buffalo were killed annually in his area.[244] To the Indian, the buffalo was a fundamental necessity to sustain life for his family and tribe. Kicking Bird, a Kiowa Chief, said of buffalo:

> ...the buffalo was their money their only resource with which to buy what they needed and did not receive from the government. The robes they could prepare and trade. They loved them just as the white man does his money, and just as it made them feel to see others killing and stealing their buffalo which were their cattle given them by the Great Father above to furnish them meat to eat and means to get things to wear...[245]

The result of the great slaughter caused the buffalo to change their migration patterns that in turn caused the Indians to change their traditional hunting grounds. The Indians became desperate, as their food supply diminished. They attacked settlements on the frontier and wagon trains

---

[243] Capps, 167
[244] Richardson, 87
[245] Ibid., 192

of emigrants heading west. This then expanded the wrath of the Americans. A delegate to Congress from Montana, James M. Cavanaugh, said, "I have never in my life seen a good Indian except when I have seen a dead Indian."[246]

In the seventeenth century Dutch scholar and jurist, Hugo Grotius, wrote: "If within the territory of a people there is any deserted and unproductive soil, this also ought to be granted to foreigners, if they ask for it. Or it is right for foreigners even to take possession of such ground, for the reason that uncultivated land ought not be considered as occupied."[247] From this, the Americans believed they had a duty if not a destiny to move into Indian lands.

Probably the most devastating curse to the Comanches was the effects of European diseases. Three diseases: cholera, measles, and smallpox were the scourge of the Plains Indians, as they had no resistance. At the time, there were no treatments to counter these diseases, but some Europeans had acquired a resistance.

In Europe, it was found that once the smallpox organism was localized, the human population would then gradually develop a resistance. Europeans had confronted smallpox for centuries and eventually developed some resistance to the disease. They were not immune, as about 40 percent of the people who acquired the disease died. The survivors, though, became immune.

President George Washington contracted smallpox when, as a young man, he had visited the Caribbean. Fortunately, Washington survived and thereby became immune. It may have seemed disastrous for Washington to

---

[246] Capps, 192
[247] Ibid., 157

have acquired smallpox. The disaster later proved providential, as Washington was never incapacitated with smallpox while leading his new nation in its most crucial period.

The Indians were not so fortunate. Once a Plains Indian acquired smallpox, he surely died. The Comancheria was sterile, as few Europeans or Americans ventured into it. Smallpox is a highly contagious disease that can only be carried by human beings. When the Americans pressed into the Comancheria, they brought smallpox with them. Perhaps in time, the Comanches would have developed a resistance to the disease as had the Europeans.

Cholera was another European disease that plagued the plains Indians. Cholera, which is caused by ingesting food or water contaminated with the cholera bacteria, causes severe dehydration after exposure. More than a pint of fluid can be lost every hour. If the fluid is not replaced, the victim may die in a few hours. The mortality rate is about 50 percent. Rwanda, in 1994, suffered a severe outbreak of cholera. More than 23,000 people died from the disease.

Measles, a highly contagious viral infection, was another European disease that devastated the Plains Indians. In America, measles was considered a childhood disease and was of little concern. Now, immunization is a requirement for school admission. In developing countries today, where immunization is absent, measles causes the deaths of more than a million people every year. The Comanches, too, had no immunization. They had no concept of the disease, and death from the disease soon followed its contraction.

For the Plains Indians, these three European diseases were much like the Black Death or bubonic plague that struck Europe in the 14th century. This plague first entered Europe in 1347 in Sicily. From here, it spread by merchant ships throughout Europe. At least 25 million Europeans died from the plague. Europe did not recover from the plague until the 16th century. Without any familiarity with the disease, people had no defense and, consequently, died. Poor sanitary conditions, prevalent at the time, contributed to the spread of the disease.

The Comanches, also, had no knowledge of the three European diseases. They had not seen them before. In time, the Comanches developed a cure for snake bites and tuberculosis. After another century, possibly, the Comanches may have developed a treatment for the three European diseases.

When Cortez first entered Mexico, the population was estimated at 30 million people. Fifty years later, the population of Mexico was estimated at three million. The population was decimated largely because of European diseases: cholera, smallpox and measles.

To die from a disease was not the warriors way of death. A Comanche warrior knew that he would die in battle; be trampled by buffalo, or in some other way while on horseback. Slowly dying in bed from a debilitation disease was totally unworthy.

In Texas, the Penateka or southern Comanches were decimated by these European diseases. In 1848, they were struck by smallpox that was then followed by a cholera attack. Their numbers suffered a massive decrease. Counted with their losses were two wise leaders: Old Owl and Santa Anna. The Penateka Comanches were then demoralized and disintegration rapidly followed. Leaderless, the remnants of the Penatekas broke-up into small bands or joined other Comanche divisions.

In time, most Comanches became exhausted because of disease and starvation. Many sought a new life on the reservation. One band, the Quahadi Comanches, refused to enter the reservation. They were led by Quanah who is better known as Quanah Parker. Quanah was a daring and successful leader. Once, he led a night raid against a cavalry unit commanded by Colonel Ronald Mackenzie who was specifically ordered to attack Quanah's band. The Comanches came away with many fine cavalry horses. On another occasion, Quanah was requested to surrender. Quanah answered, "Tell the white chiefs that the Quahadis are warriors and will surrender when the blue coats come and whip us."[248]

Quanah, himself, has an interesting history. His name means fragrant and was given to him by his white mother who was captured by the Comanches in 1836 when she was nine years old. When his mother, Cynthia Ann Parker, turned 18, Comanche Leader, Peta Nocona, chose her as his wife.[249] She bore him two sons and a daughter. In 1860, Cynthia was recaptured by a unit composed of U.S. Cavalry and Texas Rangers. She was holding her baby daughter when she was captured while her husband and two sons managed to escape. The separation from her husband and two sons was devastating for Cynthia. Living with her "own people" was not satisfying either. She still

---

[248] Ibid., 192
[249] Capps, 189 & 194

longed for her two sons. In 1864, her daughter died of a fever. Cynthia then starved herself.

Quanah retained his name given to him by his mother, although it was customary for a young warrior to change his name to reflect his feeling as a warrior in his tribe. Comanches believed that names had magical power.[250] Quanah was the quintessence of being a Comanche and a Comanche leader. He was a warrior, and a leader of his people to the end.

In time, the Quahadi Comanches with their leader, Quanah, were the only Comanche band that refused to move to the reservation. In September 1874, they along with their Kiowa and Cheyenne allies sought refuge in the Palo Duro Canyon, which is near Amarillo, Texas. The Palo Duro Canyon had always been a safe area for the Comanches. This time, however, Quanah's old nemesis, Colonel Ronald Mackenzie, surprised the Indians in the canyon and forced them to retreat.

Few Indians were killed in the attack, but they fled without most of their horses and food. As they gathered from a vantage point to launch a counterattack, they observed Colonel Mackenzie's troopers. They proceded to destroy the Indians' food and then committed the most horrendous abomination conceivable. They slaughtered the Indians' horses. There were about fourteen hundred horses killed.[251] The sight of so many dead Indian horses went beyond the bounds of Comanche tenets. The Comanches held the horse in the highest veneration. It was termed the "god dog."

---

[250] Newcomb, 167
[251] Capps, 194

With winter coming on and only a few horses plus a depleted buffalo population, Quanah rallied his people and surrendered them. This was 1875, almost two centuries after the Comanches first entered the Comancheria. Yamparika Comanche leader, Ten Bears, summed up the surrender:

> My people have never first drawn a bow or fired a gun against the whites. There has been trouble between us, and my young men have danced the war dance. But it was not begun by us. It was you who sent out the first soldier and we sent out the second... If the Texans had kept out of our country, there might have been peace.[252]

> But that which you now say we must live on is too small. The Texans have taken away the places where the grass grew the thickest and the timber was the best. Had we kept that, we might have done the things you ask. But it is too late. The white man has the country which we loved, and we only wish to wander on the prairie until we die.

Probably the biggest victors in the war with the Comanches were the Mexicans. Since Spain's defeat by the Comanches at the battle of Red River in 1759, Spain realized that the Comanches were the masters of Texas. Spain also realized that if the Comanches kept the Spaniards out of Texas, they could also keep all other invaders out. In this way, Texas would be a buffer to

---

[252] Rollings, 82

protect Northern Mexico from intruders. However, they still needed a way to keep the Comanches and Apaches from raiding Mexico. This last Mexican condition was provided by the U.S. Army and the Texas Rangers who acted for the Americans in Texas.

Winston Churchill wrote in *The World Crisis*, "The terrible Ifs accumulate."[253] If Stephen Austin had not established a colony in Texas for Americans; if Santa Anna had not been the dictator of Mexico, there might not have been an independent Texas. If the American colony in Texas had been limited to only East Texas, there would have never been a conflict between Texans and Comanches. The Comanches would have then continued raiding into Mexico.

The Comanches were a dominate force in Texas, as they controlled the western half of Texas for almost two hundred years. Spain claimed Texas for three hundred years but could never penetrate the Comancheria. Mexico claimed Texas for fifteen years, as it was part of the Spanish claim when Mexico declared its independence. Mexico like Spain was equally inept in governing Texas. France claimed Texas for six years when La Salle lost his way to the mouth of the Mississippi and instead established a colony near Texas' Matagorda Bay. La Salle's colony soon died.

The Comanches had a greater influence in the shaping of Texas than Spain, France or Mexico. Their influence is probably equal to that of Texas and the Confederacy. Texas history, to be correct, must recognize the contribution of the Comanches. If there had been no

---

[253] Churchill, Chapter XI

Comanches, Texas would be just another province like Coahuila, Nuevo Leon, Chihuahua or Tamaulipas. The Comanches forced Spain and then Mexico to permit Americans to come to Texas to shield Mexico from Comanche raids. The Mexicans contemplated that the Comanches would attack nearby American settlements in Texas rather than riding to more distant Mexico. If there had been no Comanches, there would have been no American immigrants to Texas. If there had been no American immigrants in Texas, there would have been no independent Texas. A seventh flag over Texas should be acknowledged, and it should be a Comanche flag or symbol.

BIBLIOGRAPHY

Books

Capps, Benjamin, *The Indians* by Time-Life Books, New York, New York, 1973 Time, Inc.

Churchill, Winston, *The World Crisis,* Volumn I, New York, Schribner's, 1928

Editors of Time-Life Books, *The Spanish West*, Time-Life Books, New York, New York, 1976, Time, Inc.

Foster, Morris W., *Being Comanche*, The University of Arizona Press, Tuscon & London, 1991

Frazer, Robert W., *Forts of the West,* University of Oklahoma Press, Norman & London, 1965, 1972

Johnson, William Weber and The Editors of Life, *Mexico,* Life World Library, New York, New York, 1961, Time Inc.

National Geographic Society, *Atlas of World History*, National geograph;ic Society, 1997

Griffin-Pierce, Trudy, *The Encyclopedia of Native America,* Penguin Books USA Inc., 375 Hudson Street, New York, New York 10014, USA, 1995

McDowell, Bart, *Journey Across Russia: The Soviet Uniion Today*, Special Publication Division, National Geographic Society, Washington, D.C., 1970

Nevin, David, *The Texans*, Time-Life Books, New York, New York, 1975, Time Inc.

Nevin, David, *The Soldiers*, Time-Life Books, New York, New York, 1973, 1974 Time Inc.

Newcomb, W.W. Jr., *The Indians of Texas,* University of Texas Press, Austin and London, 1961

Regan, Geoffrey, *The Guinness Book of Decisive Battles*, Canopy Books, A division of Abbeville Press, Inc., New York 1992

Richardson, Rupert Norval, *Comanche Barrier To South Plains Settlement,* Eakin Press, Austin, Texas, 1996

Rollings, Willard H., *The Comanche,* 1989, Chelsea House Publishers, New York and Philadelphia

Thomas, Hugh and the Editors of Time-Life Books, *Spain*, Life World Library, New York, New York, 1962

Walker, Paul Robert, *Trail of the Wild West,* National Geographic Society, 1997

Periodicals

Angel, Paul Tudor, "Evidence of Earth's Lost Civilization," *The Barnes Review*, Vol.IV, No. 7, September/October 1998, pp 15-27

Cox, Mike, "The Comanche War Trail: Terror in the Night," *Texas Highways*, August 1997, pp 42-49

Petit, Charles W., "Rediscovering America," *U.S. News & World Report*, October 12, 1998, pp 56-64.

Miscellaneous

"The Military History of Texas Map," Map Ink, P.O. Box 5240, Norman, Oklahoma 73070

The Seventh Flag
Comanche Indians in Texas

Compton's Home Library, The Complete Reference Collection, 1998 Edition, The Learning Company, One Athenaeum Street, Cambridge, MA 02142

John Proctor

About the Author

John Proctor was born and reared in San Antonio, Texas. Living in San Antonio meant that he was always close to an old and proud military tradition. San Antonio is not only the home of the Alamo but also Fort Sam Houston, which was established in 1879. Before this, Spain also established a fort here in 1718, which was called: Presidio of San Antonio de Bejar. During the war with Mexico, Robert E. Lee was first posted to San Antonio. The Apache Indian chief, Geronimo, when captured, was sent to Fort Sam Houston. Teddy Roosevelt, when organizing his roughriders, used the Alamo as his headquarters.

John Proctor grew-up in San Antonio when elementary school children made pilgrimages to the Alamo every year to honor the men who died for our freedom. John became convinced that Texas was a special place. There was no other place quite like it. Texas history under six flags was accepted without question.

Recently, however, John realized one of the most significant elements in Texas history was omitted. Why were Americans settlers invited to live in Texas when Texas was claimed by Spain and later Mexico? If Texas were a Spanish province, it would seem that it would have been colonized by Spain. Nevertheless, Americans were invited to come to Texas if they fulfilled two requirements: become Spanish citizens and accept the Catholic faith. The answer to the question was readily found. Texas, at the time, was a wild and dangerous place, principally because the Comanche Indians ruled Texas.

After completing public school education in San Antonio, John Proctor attended the University of Texas at Austin. While at the university, he obtained a BA degree in geology and a BS degree in Petroleum Engineering. He also entered the ROTC program at the university and received a commission as a second lieutenant in the Air Force.

After graduation from the university, John Proctor pursued two careers: the petroleum industry and the Air Force Reserve. He was on active duty in the Air Force during the Korean conflict and then remained in the Air Force Reserve for 28 years. His work as a petroleum engineer was done over a 30-year period in the oil and gas fields of Texas and New Mexico.

www.ingramcontent.com/pod-product-compliance
Lightning Source LLC
Chambersburg PA
CBHW051430280526
45785CB00003B/1229